CHRISTIANITY AND WORLD RELIGIONS
REVISED EDITION

Christianity and World Religions, Revised Edition:
Questions We Ask About Other Faiths

Christianity and World Religions
978-1-5018-7333-1
978-1-5018-8314-9 *Large Print*
978-1-5018-7334-8 *e-Book*

Christianity and World Religions: DVD
978-1-5018-7337-9

Christianity and World Religions: Leader Guide
978-1-5018-7335-5
978-1-5018-7336-2 *e-Book*

Also from Adam Hamilton

24 Hours That Changed the World

Christianity's Family Tree

Confronting the Controversies

Creed

Enough

Faithful

Final Words from the Cross

Forgiveness

Half Truths

John

Leading Beyond the Walls

Love to Stay

Making Sense of the Bible

Moses

Not a Silent Night

Revival

Seeing Gray in a World of Black and White

Selling Swimsuits in the Arctic

Speaking Well

The Call

The Journey

The Way

Unafraid

Unleashing the Word

When Christians Get It Wrong

Why?

For more information, visit www.AdamHamilton.org.

ADAM HAMILTON

Author of *Half Truths* and *Creed*

CHRISTIANITY
— AND —
WORLD RELIGIONS

REVISED EDITION

QUESTIONS WE ASK ABOUT OTHER FAITHS

Abingdon Press
Nashville

CHRISTIANITY AND WORLD RELIGIONS:
QUESTIONS WE ASK ABOUT OTHER FAITHS
REVISED EDITION

Copyright © 2005, 2018 Abingdon Press
All rights reserved.

Library of Congress Cataloging-in-Publication Data has been requested.

978-1-5018-7333-1
First edition published in 2005 as ISBN 978-0-6874-9430-9.

18 19 20 21 22 23 24 25 26 27—10 9 8 7 6 5 4 3 2 1
MANUFACTURED IN THE UNITED STATES OF AMERICA

With grateful appreciation to twentieth-century missionary
E. Stanley Jones whose book,
The Christ of the Indian Road,
captures the spirit I hope infuses this book.

CONTENTS

CONTENTS

INTRODUCTION

According to the latest Pew Research Center data, about one in three people in the world claims a Christian faith. Nearly one in four is Muslim. One in six is Hindu. One in sixteen is Buddhist. One in five hundred is Jewish. And about one in six of the world's people is unaffiliated with any religion.[1]

While Christianity is the largest religion in the world, with around 2.3 billion adherents, two-thirds of the world's population is not Christian. This fact raises certain questions for earnest Christians: If there is only one God, as Christianity asserts, and that God has revealed himself through Jesus Christ, why are there so many different religions? How does the God of Scripture view earnest followers of other faiths? What do the other religions teach and why? At what points does Christianity find common ground with them? Where do they differ? Is there anything a Christian can learn from people of other faiths? How should Christians relate to their Muslim, Hindu, Buddhist, or Jewish neighbors?

This book considers those questions and others. In each chapter, we will examine one of the world's major religions. We'll seek to understand the essential beliefs and historical setting of each faith. We'll look for common ground where we agree. And we will note, with honesty and humility, where we disagree. Along the way, we will gain a greater understanding of what Christians believe and why we believe it. Ultimately I hope this study helps us better understand our neighbors of other faiths, and in the process leads us to better fulfill the command to love our neighbor as we love ourselves.

Increasingly for Americans, our neighbors are people of other faiths. While 70 percent of Americans today claim to be Christian, 30 percent are either people of other faiths or people who claim no religious faith. That means about 100 million of our neighbors in the United States have a different faith understanding than we do. At some point, each of us will be confronted with the claims of persons of other faiths. Our children will have friends and teachers who are a part of other religions. It's likely that you already have doctors, coworkers, and friends of other faiths. If not, you will. Part of loving your neighbor is understanding them.

A first step is to move toward what scholars call a "theology of religions." That will give us a foundation for looking at other religions in our world. A theology of religions aims to answer some of the basic questions I mentioned above, questions like:

- Why are there so many different religions?
- What is the relationship between these religions?
- How does God look at people of other religions?
- What is the eternal fate of those who practice a religion other than the one I follow?

In chapter one, we'll look at these questions from a particular Christian perspective. As we'll learn, various Christians offer different answers to these questions. I approach my own study of the world's religions with an effort to be open and understanding, and with a willingness to see truth where it may be found. But the lens through which I see the world is my own Christian faith and experience.

I write as a pastor. I've studied each of the major world religions in seminary. I've read from their sacred scriptures. I've attended services, interviewed multiple leaders of each faith, and read numerous scholars in the field of religion. Having said that, my area of expertise is Christianity. I've written this book as an introduction to these other faiths from a Christian perspective. I urge you to use this study as a beginning point in your exploration of these faiths and to take the next step of reading, studying, and most of all, talking with people of other faiths. Your willingness to listen and learn from people of other religions may lead them, in turn, to be curious about your faith as well.

The Global Religious Landscape

% of world population

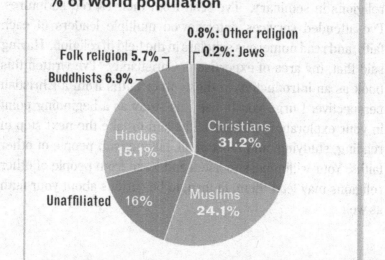

- 0.8%: Other religion
- 0.2%: Jews
- Folk religion 5.7%
- Buddhists 6.9%
- Christians 31.2%
- Hindus 15.1%
- Unaffiliated 16%
- Muslims 24.1%

Number of people, in billions

Religion	Billions
Christians	2.3B
Muslims	1.8
Unaffiliated	1.2
Hindus	1.1
Buddhists	0.5
Folk religion	0.4
Other religions	0.1
Jews	0.01

"The Changing Global Religious Landscape." Pew Research Center Demographic Study, Washington D.C. (April 5, 2017) http://www.pewforum.org/2017/04/05/the-changing-global-religious-landscape/.

PEW RESEARCH CENTER

1.

THE WISE MEN

After Jesus was born in Bethlehem in the territory of Judea during the rule of King Herod, magi came from the east to Jerusalem. They asked, "Where is the newborn king of the Jews? We've seen his star in the east, and we've come to honor him...."

[Herod] sent them to Bethlehem, saying, "Go and search carefully for the child...." When they heard the king, they went; and look, the star they had seen in the east went ahead of them until it stood over the place where the child was. When they saw the star, they were filled with joy. They entered the house and saw the child with Mary his mother. Falling to their knees, they honored him. Then they opened their treasure chests and presented him with gifts of gold, frankincense, and myrrh.

(Matthew 2:1-2, 8a, 9-11)

When I was in seminary at Southern Methodist University in Dallas, Texas, I often came back to Kansas City for visits with family. During one of those visits, I took my Grandfather Hamilton to lunch. As we were eating, he asked how my studies were going, and I told him about a course I was taking on comparative religion. I said I thought it was fascinating to learn what other people believe. I doubt that my grandfather had ever met a Hindu or a Muslim or a Buddhist. But I recall him responding to me by raising his hands and extending his two forefingers to a point, raised upward. I asked him, "What do you mean, Grandpa?"

He said, "They're all pointing in the same direction."

That was my Grandfather Hamilton's theology of religions. It was quite simple, but it captured what he believed about the other faiths, their relationship to one another and to God.

When you get down to it, everybody has a theology of religions. What is your theology of religions?

Back in 2003, I preached a series of sermons on different religions. After I had delivered the sermon on Hinduism, a man in the congregation came to me and said, "I don't understand why you're preaching these sermons. There's no need for us to hear them. All you need to tell the congregation is that everyone who has not personally accepted Jesus as their Lord and Savior is going to hell. It's that simple."

His conclusion was based upon his theology of religions. It could not have been more different from that of my Grandfather Hamilton. In this book I'm going to suggest a middle path in understanding the religions of the world, one that falls between my grandfather's view that all religions are saying the same thing (and thus are equally acceptable paths to God) and the other man's view that all the other religions are false and their adherents are condemned to hell.

14

The Hidden God

In this chapter we'll explore several of the questions a theology of religions seeks to answer, beginning with, If there is only one God, why are there so many religions? If there is only one God, wouldn't that God clearly identify himself* rather than allow confusion and multiple religions to coexist? It's an important question, and one that has left a number of people struggling with faith altogether. I'll offer one line of reasoning that makes some sense to me.

Theologians speak of *deus absconditus*—a Latin term that translates as "the hidden God." While we may see God's handiwork all around us (we ourselves are part of God's handiwork!), we are unable to see God directly. In Exodus 33, Moses prays to God, "Show me your glorious presence" to which God replies, "You can't see my face because no one can see me and live" (vv. 18, 20).

I think of the solar eclipse of 2017. We had a terrific view just outside of Kansas City. My wife, LaVon, and I, and our daughter Rebecca, drove eighty miles east of Kansas City to be in the direct path of the eclipse and to outrun the storm clouds. At just the right moment, the skies cleared. Standing in front of a cornfield, we put on our special eclipse glasses and watched the magic of the moment. It was awesome.

It struck me that this experience might shed some light on God's response to Moses' request. Our sun is a relatively modest-sized star, one of an estimated one billion, trillion stars in the universe (1,000,000,000,000,000,000,000!). God is the source of these billion, trillion stars and, presumably, God's glory and power outshine them all. We needed special solar

---

* I recognize that God is not male and the use of male pronouns can be problematic, but I retain this traditional language as using terms like "God-self" are problematic in communicating with a wide audience.

eclipse glasses to avoid being blinded by the sun. It's not hard to understand why no human could survive the experience of seeing God's glory.

We can't see God's glory directly, but in the world around us, and across the observable universe, we see God's handiwork. Religions generally agree about this. Throughout history, as people have looked at the stars or the mountains, or perceived the vastness of the seas, they said, "There has to be something more." In their hearts, they felt a presence bigger than themselves or anything they could imagine. They had what some call "intimations of glory"—feelings and experiences that we identify with God, even though we don't directly see God. God remains above, beyond, transcendent, inaccessible to our sight.

LaVon and I recently attended a gathering of people who largely were either nonreligious or nominally religious. I was the token pastor in the group. We had some meaningful conversations during the evening, and I particularly remember one with a Nobel Prize–winning physicist (who happened to be a United Methodist). I was struck by something he said: "If you want to find the atheists at a state university, go to the Religion Department. But if you want to find those who believe in God, go to the Physics Department." He got a chuckle, but he went on to explain that most of the physicists he knows are Christians. "In our field, we're used to believing in forces that are difficult to see but which shape everything that exists. We cannot see these forces directly, but we see the impact of them all around us."

I think of God in some ways as the physicist describes the four fundamental forces in nature: gravity, the electromagnetic force, the strong force, and the weak force. These forces are what make our universe possible down to the subatomic level. Though we cannot see these forces, our universe would not exist without them. We are utterly dependent upon them.

God is the force, power, and intellect that brought all of these other forces into being. Like the other four, God is unseen. And, like the other four, without God, people of faith believe we would not be alive. As the Apostle Paul, quoting the Greek philosophers and poets, summed it up: "In him we live and move and have our being" (Acts 17:28 NRSV). Apart from God we would not exist.

The words to a hymn that I love capture the idea of the hiddenness of God: "Immortal, invisible, God only wise, in light inaccessible, hid from our eyes."[2] If God, like the four foundational forces of the universe, is invisible, then we, like the scientists, are left to surmise what God is like by our observations and our experiences of God (which include God's efforts to reveal himself to us). Is it any wonder there are different religions that developed with different ways of understanding God? Or that there should be so many points at which many of the religions agree?

Feeling the Elephant

As with scientific theories, some religious ideas garner little support. Others seem to hold sway for a time, or in particular places, but eventually fade. Other ideas endure, expressing for many people over a long period of time their experiences of and reflections about God. These enduring faiths, at least four of them, are the "world religions" we're studying in this book. At the center of each of these faiths are people seeking to express the nature of ultimate reality—various writers of the Hindu scriptures, the Buddha, Moses, Muhammad, and Jesus. They all sought to understand and teach about the "something more" behind the universe, God, and what it means to be human. Each, aside from the Buddha, sought to know the hidden God.

17

A familiar metaphor to help us think about this natural variation in the world's religions comes out of a parable in ancient Buddhism. In the parable, a group of blind men encountered an elephant for the first time. They had never met one before, and their lack of sight prevented them from understanding what an elephant looks like. So they put their hands on the elephant and tried to describe its shape and form to one another.

One man, whose hands landed upon the elephant's trunk, said the creature is like a thick snake. Another, who felt only an ear, contradicted the first man and said the elephant is actually like a giant fan. A third, who grasped the elephant's side, said the animal was like a wall. Yet another, who felt the leg, said the elephant was actually a pillar as thick as a tree trunk. Another, who felt only the tail, said the elephant was shaped like a rope. The last of the men, feeling a tusk, said that elephants had a hard exoskeleton. In this way, each man, limited by his own narrow perspective, described only one aspect of the creature but thought he was describing the entire elephant. And they arrived at very different understandings based on what they experienced.

In a sense, the world's religions are like each of the blind men—attempts of human beings to describe what they cannot see in the light of what they have experienced and observed. But the hiddenness of God means that they, as Saint Paul noted, "see a reflection in a mirror." They are seeking to describe the same reality, but they offer somewhat different descriptions.

Come Find Me

While Christians believe that God may be hidden from direct view, they also believe that the hidden God wants to be found. When our four-year-old granddaughter comes to our house, she

loves to play a certain game over and over. You would recognize
it as hide-and-seek. Stella calls it "come find me." She counts
to ten while I go and hide, and then she comes looking for me.
After a couple of minutes, I'll give hints about where I am. If she
still can't find me, I'll shout, "Stella, I'm in here!" Finally she
comes and finds me. Then we'll switch places, and Stella will
hide. She can't stand to remain hidden for more than about a
minute or two. Soon she'll run out from wherever she was hid-
ing and jump into my arms, giggling with glee. She wanted to
be found. And that's the point: for Stella the joy is in the finding
and being found. In a sense, the hidden God has been constantly
inviting humanity to "come find me," dropping hints through
the natural world and the intimations of glory—the experiences
people have of God.

Christians and Jews believe that the hidden God has revealed
himself through a unique relationship with Abraham and Sarah
and their descendants. Their story, and their reflections on their
experiences of God and what they perceived about God's will,
are recorded in the Hebrew Bible—what Christians call the Old
Testament.

Christians believe that the hidden God, seeking to be found,
known, and understood, came to us "in the flesh" in Jesus Christ.
We call this the "incarnation" or enfleshment of God. Every
Christmas Eve, as we celebrate the birth of Jesus, our church
reads the prologue to John's Gospel:

In the beginning was the Word
and the Word was with God
and the Word was God....
The Word became flesh
and made his home among us.

19

We have seen his glory,
glory like that of a father's only son,
full of grace and truth.
(John 1:1, 14)

This is a central claim of the Christian faith: that God came to the world, as one of us, to reveal himself to us. Jesus taught us not only that there is a God but what God is like. He showed us God's character by his compassion for the sick, the injured, and the poor. In his suffering and death, he taught us something about our brokenness and God's grace. And in his resurrection, he taught us that God's love triumphs over every act of suffering and pain. In all of these things, God said to us, "This is who and what I am; come find me." This is why Jesus said, "Whoever has seen me has seen the Father" (John 14:9). And it is why Paul wrote of Jesus, "The Son is the image of the invisible God" (Colossians 1:15).

In many of the world's religions, Jesus is seen as a great teacher or prophet, but not as the incarnation of God. Muslims believe God's definitive revelation or word is the Quran, dictated by the angel Gabriel to Muhammad. For Buddhists, the truth about life and its meaning came through Buddha's insights at the moment of his enlightenment and his reflections following this. For Hindus, God is revealed through various stories of deities—incarnations of Brahman—and the reflections on these stories found in the Hindu scriptures.

As a Christian I believe God, who created the universe, came to us in Jesus to show us that he exists, what he is like, and what is God's will for our lives. I can make the case for this, as I will in the final chapter, but I cannot prove it. In the end, faith is a decision. Comparing the various faiths, seeing them through the eyes of their adherents, and finding good in them and points of common ground has not changed my convictions that Jesus is the definitive Word from God—the only Savior, Son, Lord. If anything, it has deepened these convictions. But studying the other faiths has led me to a greater love of those of other faiths and a deeper appreciation for why they believe what they believe. Ultimately it has also led me to a deeper understanding of my own faith.

How Does God View People of Other Faiths?

To answer the question of how God views earnest, faithful people of non-Christian religions, Christians find answers in our Scriptures, and the answers may surprise us. In the Hebrew Bible, the Christian Old Testament, non-Jews are referred to as "the nations." The Hebrew root is *goy* and some variation of it appears over 500 times in the Old Testament. It often refers to non-Israelites who did not embrace Israel's faith. Reading through all of these passages tells us a great deal about God's perspective on people who worship other gods.

First, God is seen as king of all the *nations*. In making a covenant with Abraham, God told him, "All the families of the earth will be blessed because of you" (Genesis 12:3). Later, God tells him that "all the nations of the earth will be blessed because of your descendants" (Genesis 22:18). While God had a unique relationship with Israel, it is also clear that God was concerned about all of the other nations of the ancient Near East and wanted to bless them.

The first of the Ten Commandments that God gave to Moses was, "You must have no other gods before me" (Exodus 20:3). Why? Because God is the only true God. The second commandment prohibited the Israelites from making graven images of God. Why? Because nothing made by human hands

21

could convey the glory of God, and humans found themselves all too willing to substitute idols for the living God.

God told the Israelites, "I...am a jealous God" (Exodus 20:5 NIV). God had chosen them and didn't want them to turn away to other gods. Why? As the Israelites gradually came to understand, God chose them for a special mission; they were, as a nation, intended to reveal to the *nations* of the earth God's glory, love, and purposes. The prophet Isaiah repeatedly notes that God intended Israel to be a "light to the *nations*." God intended the nations to walk in Israel's light. All of which points to a concern for those who did not yet know God.

Isaiah even wrote of a day when all the nations would be drawn to Zion, the mount on which the Temple stood, and the world would live in the light of God. There would be no more suffering, no more war, no more death. Nations would beat their swords into plows for growing crops—they would help feed their fellow humans instead of killing them—and they would bend their spears into pruning hooks to tend orchards whose fruit trees would nourish everyone.

The point I want you to notice is that repeatedly God expresses concern for non-Israelites. They mattered to God, and God intended Israel to serve as a light for them.

This is the central point of the wonderful prophetic parable, the short story of Jonah who spent three days in the belly of a big fish. You may remember that Jonah was called by God to preach repentance to the city of Nineveh, the capital of the Assyrian Empire. Jonah refused to go, but eventually relented, preached to the Ninevites, and then moped when the people actually repented and God showed them mercy. Whether you read the story as literal history or as a parable, the point of the story is the same. It is captured in the final verse of the book, where God says to Jonah, "Can't I pity Nineveh, that great city, in which there are more than one hundred twenty thousand people who can't tell their right hand from their left, and also many animals?" (Jonah 4:11).

Again and again we find this concern for the nations in the Hebrew Bible. And we find God working in and through these nations, as well as demonstrating a surprising patience toward them.

The New Testament very quickly makes the same point. Matthew's telling of the birth of Jesus is very brief (no angels, shepherds, or stable in Matthew; we have Luke to thank for these details). But Matthew does take the time to tell us that God beckoned "magi from the east" to pay homage and present their gifts to the newborn king.

Throughout the Christian world, this story is read on Epiphany weekend, which traditionally marks the arrival of the magi. Epiphany means a revelation or manifestation, specifically involving God—a moment when the invisible God becomes visible. And that is what happens in this story.

The magi (traditionally presumed to be three due to the number of gifts mentioned, though Matthew does not give us an actual number) came from somewhere in modern-day Iran. To get to Jerusalem, and then to nearby Bethlehem, they would have traveled twelve hundred miles along the Fertile Crescent. Many experts suggest that the journey might have taken two months or more.

Who were these magi, these wise men, that God beckoned by a star to come see the newborn king? The term in the Greek New Testament is *magoi* (which is also the root for our English words *magic* and *magician*). Our best sources from the ancient world portray magi as a caste of religious experts—priests—from the Zoroastrian religion. They studied the stars, and they worshiped a God called Ahura Mazda. Like the Jews, they were monotheists, and they shared a strong sense of justice and an emphasis on ethics.

What does it say about God's view of people of other religions that he invited these Zoroastrian priests to Bethlehem to be, at least in Matthew's Gospel, the first to see the newborn king? Though the Bible frowns upon astrology, God spoke to these astrologers by means of a star. But notice, too, that these followers of Ahura Mazda traveled for months bearing gifts of gold, frankincense, and myrrh in order to honor the newborn king of the Jews, gifts that likely sustained the Holy Family on their flight to Egypt. We have no evidence that the magi converted to Judaism, and there was no Christianity yet to which they might become adherents. But they surely were affected by this dramatic experience.

I wonder why God chose the Zoroastrian magi from so far away? Surely there were Jews with gold, frankincense, and myrrh in nearby Jerusalem that God might have invited, through an angel, and who would have come to see the Christ Child. At the very least, it appears that God knew the hearts of these followers of Ahura Mazda, twelve hundred miles away, and God sought to bless them and use them to accomplish his purposes. Is it possible that this story is meant to tell us about God's mercy and love for people of other faiths? And to instill in the hearts of Christians a love for these magi as well, pointing towards the kind of love Christians might have for people of other faiths? And what does it say about these Persian priests, that they followed the star, traveling for months, bearing their gifts, all to honor the birth of a long-awaited Jewish king? I think this story was meant to help us understand that there is a wideness to God's mercy—wider, perhaps, than we've often understood.

I'd like to end this chapter by offering three broad perspectives people who identify as Christians have held regarding people of other faiths.

The Religious Pluralist Perspective

Some Christians share the basic view of my Grandfather Hamilton: that the various religions are all pointing to the same ultimate reality, even if they use different metaphors, symbols, and theological ideas to describe this ultimate reality. Further, they believe that the adherents of all the religions, as well as those who have no religion and those who reject belief in God, will all ultimately be reconciled to God through Jesus Christ. This view is known as *Christian universalism*.

Unitarian Universalism, which emerged within Christianity, takes this view one step further by suggesting that a variety of religious traditions, including atheism and agnosticism, are acceptable paths to the truth. Universal salvation in this view is not a result of Christ's work, for Christ is one among many equally valid paths to the truth. This view is referred to as *religious pluralism*.

I'm not doing justice to this view, as there are nuances and distinct emphases among different pluralists and universalists. But for many pluralists, there is a tendency to see the various major world religions we'll study in this book as equally valid paths. A religion may be true for some, while another view will be true for others.

I think it is true that all of the major religions we'll consider in this book are trying to ask many of the same fundamental questions. What does it mean to be human? Is there a God? What is God like? What is the nature of ultimate reality? What happens to us when we die? How do we deal with suffering and live with hope?

But these religions are not all giving the same answers to those questions. At points, the answers are quite contradictory. And it does not honor those religions and their adherents to say

25

that all the religions are saying the same thing. Many of us are saying *some* of the same things, or at least very similar things. But at other very important points, the religions are saying quite different things. It is precisely here that I struggle with the generous spirit of religious pluralism. I love the kindness and broad spirit of this view, but by treating each religion as though it were making equally valid truth claims, it strikes me as illogical. By doing so, it fails to honor the truth claims of any of the religions.

The Exclusivist Perspective

On the opposite end of the spectrum from religious pluralism is *Christian exclusivism*. It asserts that there is only one true path to God—namely through Jesus Christ, who is the "way, the truth, and the life"—*and* that those who do not personally accept Christ as their Savior are condemned to hell. As we will see in a moment, this view is not defined simply by the idea that Christ is the only Savior of the world, and the way, the truth, and the life. It is also characterized by the notion that because this is true, all others who don't acknowledge Christ as Savior will be tormented in hell for eternity.

The exclusivist points to Scriptures like John 14:6, where Jesus says, "I am the way, the truth, and the life. No one comes to the Father except through me," or Peter's words in Acts 4:12—"Throughout the whole world, no other name has been given among humans through which we must be saved"—as evidence that non-Christians will be excluded from heaven.

Yet even these persons often leave some wiggle room. Among the questions often asked of these persons is the classic example of the people on a "remote island" who never had the opportunity to hear the gospel of Christ. Will they spend eternity in hell? The former member I mentioned earlier answered that yes, the nonbelievers on the proverbial remote island would be condemned to hell because their sin separated them from God and they had not received Christ as their Savior. But not all exclusivists take such a position. Many would allow that God judges such persons based upon the "light they had access to," meaning how they responded to what they could know of God.

Even the man I spoke to, who believed all adults who did not receive Christ would be consigned to hell, made an exception for little children who were too young to receive Christ, noting that they had not reached what he and others often call an "age of accountability," meaning that they were too young to be held accountable for understanding or choosing Christ. There was his wiggle room. I pushed him a bit, asking if the little children were saved by God's grace because they were too young to understand, was it possible that this same principle might apply to others who had never heard, or perhaps could not understand, the gospel as it was presented to them?

Christian Inclusivism

Most mainline Protestants, Roman Catholics, and a sizable number of evangelicals reject the idea of *Christian exclusivism* in favor of a view called *Christian inclusivism*. According to this view, Jesus is the only Savior of the world. No one comes to the Father except by his saving work. But here's where inclusivism makes a decisive break from exclusivism—this view insists that Jesus' saving grace can be given to whomever God chooses based upon the criteria God chooses.

As Paul explains it in the New Testament, all human beings are sinners who fall short of the glory of God. We are delivered from our sin and judgment not by anything we have done or can do, but by the free gift of grace from God. It is not a gift we deserve, nor can we earn it, but by faith we can accept that grace and let it work within us so that it changes our lives and affects the lives of those around us. We don't even need a boundless faith to accept the gift of saving grace; Jesus spoke of having faith the size of a mustard seed.

If saving grace is a gift, and God's generosity is boundless, then, the inclusivist suggests, it is possible that God may give the salvation Jesus wrought by his life, death, and resurrection to anyone God chooses based upon what God sees in this person's heart—in essence, based upon the faith that they do have.

Christian inclusivists believe that, at death, every human stands before Christ: Hindus, Buddhists, Muslims, Jews, and Christians alike. In that moment, even those who followed other faiths will realize that Jesus was in fact the Savior they had been seeking their whole lives; they simply did not recognize him until then. This is the picture we have in Paul's words in Romans 14:11-12, when he paraphrases Isaiah 45:23: "It is written, 'As I live, says the Lord, *every* knee will bow to me, and *every* tongue will give praise to God'" (emphasis added).

Christian inclusivists believe this is what Revelation describes in the end of the Bible when it speaks of the new heaven and the new earth, and how in that place, "The nations will walk by its light, and the kings of the earth will bring their glory into it. Its gates will never be shut by day, and there will be no night there. They will bring the glory and honor of the nations into it" (Revelation 21:24-26).

Inclusivism is seen by many people as the view of some of the early church fathers. Many people believe it was the view of John Wesley. It was the view of C. S. Lewis, John R. W. Stott, and many other evangelicals, just as it is the view of many mainline Christians and Roman Catholics today. Note this does not mean that everyone will be "saved." But it appears in Scripture that many who sought to know and love God, but who did not know Christ, will, in the end, bow before him and receive the gift of his saving grace.

I've been asked from time to time: If faithful people of other faiths might enter heaven, why do we bother to share the gospel? I don't share the message of Christ with people of other faiths because I'm afraid that they will be tormented for all eternity if they don't say yes to Jesus. I share the gospel because I believe it is true, and if it is true that in Christ God came to us, then Christ offers the definitive truth about God and the definitive truth about ourselves. In him we find grace and mercy, light and life, hope and joy. I share the gospel because I think it offers the clearest picture of who God is and what God wills for our lives.

Loving Through Understanding

In a world where there is so much conflict over religion, I think it is critically important for Christians to come to understand our non-Christian neighbors better, so that we can better love them as we love ourselves.

In a world where two out of every three human beings are not Christian, we have to figure this out if we're going to keep our world from continued hostility and conflict over religion. We have to get to know one another better so that we can fulfill what Jesus called the second great commandment. And it is really not so difficult. It's as easy as breaking bread and sharing stories. In the process of doing so, you may find yourself growing as a Christian. You might just meet your own magi, or you might play the role of the magi for someone else.

C. S. Lewis powerfully captured the idea of inclusivism in the final installment of his children's novels, the *Chronicles of Narnia*. In these stories, Jesus is portrayed as the magnificent

29

lion, Aslan. At the end of this seven-volume series of novels, Aslan returns for the last judgment. As the judgment begins, Emeth, a follower of another god, comes face to face with Aslan. Upon seeing Aslan, Emeth realizes that he has followed the wrong god his entire life. He falls on his face, anticipating he'll be destroyed. Listen to how Emeth describes what happens next:

> The Glorious One bent down his golden head and touched my forehead...and said, "Son, thou art welcome." But I said, "Alas, Lord, I am no son of thine but the servant of [another god]." He answered, "Child, all the service thou hast done to [your god], I account as service done to me." Then...I...questioned the Glorious One and said, "Lord, is it then true...that thou and [the other god] are one?" The Lion growled...and said, "It is false."...I said...."Yet I have been seeking [the other god] all my days." "Beloved," said the Glorious One, "unless thy desire had been for me thou wouldst not have sought so long and so truly. For all find what they truly seek."[3]

This picture of the grace of God in Jesus Christ strikes me as profoundly biblical. It is what I see of the heart of God when I look at the story of God inviting the magi to come and see. God continues to beckon us today to show the mercy he showed, even as he invites all the world to "come find me."

Timeline
Hinduism and Christianity

Dates	Hinduism	Christianity
2000 BC	Migration to the Indus River Valley (3000-2000 BC)	Abraham and Sarah (ca. 2000 BC)
1500 BC	Vedas composed and passed down orally (2000-1000 BC)	Moses leads the Israelites out of slavery in Egypt (+/-1300 BC)
1000 BC	Vedas committed to writing (1000 BC)	King David (ca. 1000 BC)
	Earliest Upanishads composed (600 BC)	Hebrew prophets (850-450 BC)
500 BC	Bhagavad Gita written (550-500 BC)	Babylonian Exile (586-539 BC)
0		Life of Jesus (4 BC-AD 29)

2.

HINDUISM

At one time you were like a dead person because of the things you did wrong and your offenses against God…so that you were children headed for punishment just like everyone else.

However, God is rich in mercy. He brought us to life with Christ while we were dead as a result of those things that we did wrong. He did this because of the great love that he has for us. You are saved by God's grace! And God raised us up and seated us in the heavens with Christ Jesus. God did this to show future generations the greatness of his grace by the goodness that God has shown us in Christ Jesus.

You are saved by God's grace because of your faith. This salvation is God's gift. It's not something you possessed. It's not something you did that you can be proud of. Instead, we are God's accomplishment, created in Christ Jesus to do good things. God planned for these good things to be the way that we live our lives.

(Ephesians 2:1-10)

33

In February 2017, we were shocked by a hate crime that took place in Olathe, Kansas, a suburb just a few miles from the church that I serve in the Kansas City area. Fifty-one-year-old Adam Purinton walked into Austin's Bar and Grill and began to harass two Indian men, engineers who had just gotten off work from their jobs at Garmin, a large tech company headquartered just down the street. When Purinton continued with the verbal assault, restaurant staff asked him to leave. He left, but returned shortly with a gun and proceeded to shoot the two Indian men and another man who came to their aid. One of the men, thirty-two-year-old Srinivas Kuchibhotla, was killed.

In the aftermath of the killing of her husband, Sunayana Dumala, Kuchibhotla's widow, made this plea on Facebook. "Take some time to understand and embrace diversity in race, culture, and religion," she wrote. "It is in our hands to make our society safe and secure for our future generations and create a fearless world."[1] Powerful words coming from a woman who had just lost her husband in a racial and likely religiously motivated hate crime.

What Christian would not wish for all people to be able to live in a world without fear? If we are to work toward that goal, we must first understand the people who are our neighbors of other faiths. What do they believe? Why do they believe it? Where do we find common ground? Understanding even the basics of their religion gives us the basis for meaningful conversation and the opportunity to better love our neighbors as we love ourselves.

Hinduism from a Historical Perspective

In this chapter, we turn to Hinduism, the dominant religion of Kuchibhotla's home country of India. Hindus consider their religion the oldest living faith in the world. Hinduism certainly has ancient roots. Those roots go back between two thousand and three thousand years before Christ, when various tribal groups migrated into the Indus River Valley—what is today northern India. They were part of a larger group of people known as Proto-Indo-Europeans or Aryans. Some of them eventually made their way into Central Asia and even to the western edge of Europe (the name for Iran is derived from the word Aryan). These peoples once shared a common language and religious beliefs. Though these evolved differently in the east and west, parallels can be seen between the deities of the Greco-Roman myths and the deities of Hinduism.

Hinduism's holy writings include the Vedas—hymns, liturgies, and direction for the ritual sacrifices of ancient Hinduism. The Vedas were composed and passed on orally from around 2000 BC and committed to writing perhaps as early as 1000 BC. Later, perhaps as early as the 600s BC, if not earlier, a second body of work was composed, called the Upanishads. These are technically considered part of the Vedas, but serve both as commentary and as the summation of Hindu philosophy. These are the most important of Hinduism's scriptures. Their composition continued long after the time of Christ. Some are written as short verses, something like the Proverbs of the Old Testament. Others are extended conversations. Like the Proverbs, they take the form of poetry. They were written, as noted above, beginning sometime around the year 600 BC and continued to be composed well after the time of Christ.

The best-known section of the Upanishads, and the most important text for Hindus, is called the Bhagavad Gita. It was written shortly after the Israelites returned from the Babylonian Exile (539 BC). The book, about the length of two of our Gospels, is a short portion of a much longer poem that runs about 100,000 verses (making it the longest poem in human history). The

Bhagavad Gita records a conversation between Arjuna, a young prince, and his charioteer (who is an incarnation of the divine Krishna). Arjuna is the rightful heir to the throne, which has been safeguarded by Arjuna's uncle until Arjuna comes of age. Now Arjuna's uncle wants to place his own son on the throne rather than giving it to Arjuna. Thus, Arjuna has been placed in a position of waging war against his uncle. Arjuna would rather give up his claim to the throne than to go to war with his own kin. But Krishna encourages him to do his duty and fight for his throne.

Arjuna poses questions about the meaning of life. In response, Krishna offers answers that call Arjuna and all humanity to self-sacrifice and the pursuit of wisdom. In this way, the beautiful poetry of the Bhagavad Gita encapsulates some of the central tenets of Hinduism. No Hindu home would be without a copy of this sacred book.

As seen in the chart at the beginning of this chapter, Abraham and Sarah lived about the time the Vedas were being composed (around 2000 BC—but keep in mind, there's uncertainty about when to date Abraham and Sarah, just as there is about when the Vedas were composed). Moses led the children of Israel out of slavery in Egypt in the 1200s BC (though some say earlier). King David composed his psalms about the time the Vedas were committed to writing—about 1000 BC. The Upanishads were written starting around the time of the various Hebrew prophets in the Bible and continued to be composed after the time of Christ.

What Hindus Believe

It's impossible to convey the breadth of Hindu beliefs in this short chapter, but I'd like to describe a few of the essential tenets of Hinduism as I understand them. You may want to explore others on your own. (And as a disclaimer, we should note here that not all Hindus are of the same mind in terms of how they talk about their faith. That shouldn't be surprising; Christians don't all describe their faith in the same way either. If you were to interview a Russian Orthodox priest and ask him to describe Christianity, and then you asked a Pentecostal pastor to do the same, you'd get somewhat or likely very different responses.)

One Transpersonal God but Multiple Deities

Christians are often surprised to learn that Hindus believe in one God, most often referred to as Brahman. This is confusing to Christians, as Hindus speak of a variety of "deities." But Hindus hold that all of these deities (as many as 330 million by some accounts) are only manifestations of the one supreme God who created all things. Hindus speak of God in the singular, and Hindu scriptures say that there is only one true God.

As a local Hindu leader explained it to me several years ago, the one god manifests himself in ways that human beings can understand. Sometimes, Brahman can appear as a human, as was the case when Krishna appeared as Arjuna's charioteer (think of movies like the *Oh God!* films of the late 1970s and early 1980s in which God was portrayed by actor George Burns, or the 2003 film, *Bruce Almighty*, in which God is played by Morgan Freeman. In these films the one God simply takes the form of a human in order to reveal himself to certain people. Some of the incarnations of God described in Hinduism are believed to have literally occurred, while others are clearly mythological.

If you witness worship in a Hindu temple, you'll see a number of statues of important Hindu deities. You'll hear the sound of chanting and the ringing of a bell. You will see a fire offering made to the deities, waved in front of the faces of their statues.

37

You'll smell incense, and you'll see food offered to the deities. After worship, the people eat the food they've offered.

When I visited a Hindu worship service, I was offered an apple that had first been offered to one of the deities. I was reminded of Paul's First Letter to the Corinthians in which he addressed the question of whether Christians in Corinth could, in good conscience, eat meat that had been sacrificed to the various deities in Corinth, then sold in the marketplace. Paul reassured them; since we Christians don't believe that these idols are actual gods, it's fine to eat food that had first been sacrificed to these deities. But, he noted, if it troubled one's conscience or made another believer stumble, the believer was to refrain from eating it. My experience at the Hindu temple helped me more deeply understand what Paul was saying.

In Hinduism, God or Brahman is both transcendent and immanent; that is, God is both beyond or above the created universe, and at the same time, God permeates the universe, and the universe itself is part of God. God in Hinduism transcends personality and our capacity to understand or comprehend. For this reason, many Hindus see Brahman as impersonal—or, perhaps more accurately, *beyond* personal, and hence the various deities or incarnations are essential in comprehending and connecting with God. That view is in stark contrast with Judaism and Christianity, which hold that God is personal, knowable, and that it is possible to have a deeply personal experience of and relationship with God.

To illustrate the point, I once asked a Hindu leader whether he felt a closeness to God. He told me that only those much further along the spiritual path could hope to feel such a connection to Brahman.

Hindus also believe that everything that exists is in some sense part of God—though God is greater than the everything else that exists. Even a person's soul, according to Hinduism, is in some sense God. Christians and Jews see this differently. To them, while everything that exists is God's handiwork, God stands apart from creation. God made the mountains, but the mountains are not part of God.

Every Creature Has a Soul That Is Reincarnated

In Hinduism, every creature—human beings and animals alike—has a soul, called the *atman*. Hindus believe that the *atman* is the true self, beyond the ego or false self. Because Hinduism teaches that everything is part of the supreme God, the *atman*, like the rest of creation, is divine. It originates with God before it begins its journey on earth. Its ultimate desire and destiny is to be completely reunited to God.

For Hindus, the soul's journey on earth begins in the form of an animal, or perhaps even a plant. To be reunited with God, the soul needs to gain the spiritual knowledge to let go of ego and of this life and to fulfill its duty to God. The Hindu word for that duty is *dharma*. It includes acts of kindness, compassion, mercy, and love. Even souls in animal form have this duty insofar as they are capable of performing it. If the soul lives out its *dharma*, it has a chance to be reincarnated as a higher life form.

Because they have divinity within themselves, Hindus believe, they are not born sinners. The problem with humans isn't sin, but ignorance. Humans may be ignorant of the divine spirit within them, of God, or of their *dharma,* and as a result they cling to this life, act in ways that are not according to their duty, and consequently bring pain upon themselves or to others. The human struggle thus is not to overcome sin but to overcome a lack of knowledge, a process that may take many lifetimes.

We are born, we learn, we die, and then we are reborn. Souls strive to gain knowledge and fulfill their duty to move ever close to God. If the lessons one was intended to learn were not learned, and the individual committed bad deeds and was driven by evil motives, the person will carry this negative account with him or her into the next life, being reborn in a less fortuitous situation, possibly even as a lower life form—a bit like flunking a grade in school. But if the person's life was characterized by good deeds, the individual created good energy that follows him or her into the next life. The word *karma* is used in Hinduism to describe the good or bad we bring with us into the next life, based upon our good or bad deeds or intentions in this life. *Karma* is also used to describe this principle of causality—that what we do in this life determines our fate in the next life, popularly summarized by the phrase "what goes around, comes around."

Hindus call this long, nearly endless cycle of birth, life, death, and rebirth *samsara*. According to Hinduism, as a human being you already have been through countless reincarnations just to reach this point, starting as a very primitive form of life and evolving, and then perhaps experiencing many human lives. And then one day, perhaps after hundreds or even thousands of lifetimes, you finally reach a state where you have shed your ego and your clinging to the things of this life, and you are reunited with God upon your death. Hindus call this final release *moksha*. Some describe it as a drop of water being reunited with the ocean. Others simply see it as being reunited with God. The word for this final state is *nirvana*—which is being absorbed by or becoming one with God.

Nonviolence: Ahimsa

There is one more important concept in Hinduism that is important to note: the concept of *ahimsa*. Like many other things, Hindus have varied interpretations of the meaning of this term, but the basic concept is "noninjury." Hindus are not

40

to injure other living things, including themselves. This is why many Hindus are vegetarians. But, as I noted, this principle is interpreted differently by different Hindus, which is why many Hindus do eat meat.

Ahimsa also leads many Hindus to be pacifists, though others accept the concept of a "just war." Mohandas Gandhi (or as he came to be called, Mahatma, a title of respect that means "great-souled") was surely the best known Hindu of the previous century. He was most famous for the way he championed the concept of nonviolent resistance—another expression of *ahimsa*.

Points of Connection

Ahimsa as nonviolence or noninjury should sound familiar to Christians. Jesus taught the same when he told his disciples to "turn the other cheek" and to "love your enemies," and he demonstrated it when he refused to take up arms against the crowd that came to arrest him and those who planned to crucify him. Paul captures the same idea when he writes, "Do not repay anyone evil for evil," but instead, "overcome evil with good" (Romans 12:17, 21 NIV).

In addition to this connection between *ahimsa* and Christian nonviolence, there are many other points of connection between the Hindu and Christian faiths. At the center of both faiths is the belief in one Supreme Being. Listen to how Arjuna describes God in the Bhagavad Gita: "I see the splendor of an infinite beauty which illumines the whole universe. It is thee! with thy crown and scepter. How difficult thou art to see! But I see thee: as fire, as the sun, blinding, incomprehensible....Heaven and earth and all the infinite spaces are filled with thy Spirit and before the wonder of thy fearful majesty the worlds tremble" (Bhagavad Gita 11:17, 20).

41

That verse sounds very much like the descriptions of God we find in the Bible—I think of the vision Isaiah had of God in Isaiah 6:1-8, or the glorious images of God as described in Revelation. It also reminds me of some of the great hymns of the Christian faith.

It's also interesting that at the very point where our views of God seem most to diverge, the idea of the various "deities" revered in Hinduism, there is a connection. For Hindus, these deities or incarnations are moments when Brahman appeared in human or animal form in order to reveal his will to humanity. I'm reminded of an interesting passage in Genesis 18 where three "men" call upon Abraham and Sarah. The biblical author refers to these three, collectively, as "the Lord." Of course, at the center of the Christian faith is the idea that God did not simply appear to be human, but came to us as a human in Jesus Christ.

It's also clear that Hindus and Christians share a belief that humans were meant to live lives of love, compassion, and kindness, and that practicing good deeds is meant to be our way of life. The command to love one's neighbor and Jesus' parables of the good Samaritan and the sheep and the goats capture values that are important to Hindus as well.

Points of Divergence

Let's consider a few of the places where Christianity and Hinduism diverge, places where we simply disagree.

God

As I read about Brahman as Hindus conceive of it, I was in some ways reminded of how God revealed himself to Moses. When Moses asked for God's name, God said, "I Am Who I Am" (Exodus 3:14). I've always read this divine name as God's way of saying, "I am being itself. Everything that exists derives its existence from me." For Jews and Christians, everything is contingent upon God. When Paul says to the Athenians, "In him we live and move and have our being"—quoting the Greek poet Epimenides—he's expressing an idea that parallels the Hindu understanding of God (Acts 17:28 NRSV).

But at other points, Hinduism's conception of God seems to diverge significantly from the biblical understanding of God. For example, while Brahman can be manifest in personal ways, God in Hinduism is conceived in very impersonal terms. Jewish and Christian Scriptures represent God much differently.

From the beginning, God created human beings for relationship with him, to be recipients of God's love. In the early chapters of Genesis, God walks through the garden of Eden each evening and talks with Adam and Eve. Moses and David both spoke to and of God in intensely personal ways. Jesus referred to God as his Father, taught his disciples to address God as Abba, and told parables in which he described God in very personal ways. God was the loving and merciful father to prodigal children, the loving shepherd who searches for lost sheep, and the generous employer paying his employees more than they deserved.

While the Hindu I spoke with several years ago couldn't imagine personally experiencing God, every Christian from the time they are children speaks of and sings to God in personal terms, and most have profoundly personal experiences of God at various times in their lives (for many, this is a daily occurrence).

Our conception of God also differs as it relates to how we conceive of God's relationship to creation. In traditional Christianity, God is the Creator, and is present everywhere, but the creation is not God or somehow part of God. God dwells in the human soul by the Holy Spirit, but the Holy Spirit and the human soul are never one and the same, despite our mystical union with God. This is different from Hinduism's pantheism (God is equated with the creation so that each creature is part of God) or, in some expressions of Hinduism, panentheism (the idea that everything is a part of God, yet God is more than creation and transcends creation).

The distinction between Christianity and Hinduism at this point is perhaps best expressed in the following illustration: If I were to take you to the Nelson-Atkins Art Museum in Kansas City to see an exhibit of Pablo Picasso's paintings, and if I then pointed to one of the canvases and said, "Look, there's Pablo Picasso," you would probably be confused. The painting was created by Pablo Picasso. It reflects his skills, abilities, imagination, values, character, and beliefs, but it is still only a painting by the artist, not the artist himself. In the same way, Christians believe the universe is God's handiwork, God's presence permeates everything, and everything that exists reflects in some way the glory of God. But God is not the creation, but instead its Creator.

As it relates to the idea of God's incarnation, while Hindus and Christians both recognize that God has occasionally appeared in human form, Christians look upon Jesus as God in a way that Hindus would not. We believe that something of the very essence of God became incarnate—was conceived, born, lived, and died in the flesh in Jesus. The creeds note that Jesus was fully divine and yet fully human. In Jesus God actually became flesh; Jesus was born, lived, died, and rose again. God may have appeared in human form on other occasions, but for Christians Jesus was the only *incarnation* of God.

Reincarnation and Salvation

While there are other differences between Hindus and Christians, among the most significant differences are our conceptions of what happens to us after our death, what salvation looks like, and what we need to be saved *from*.

For Hindus, the problem with the human condition is ignorance that leads us to live ego-centered lives that bring suffering to ourselves and others. The key to deliverance is knowledge, which is gained over many lifetimes. It is their pursuit of good works and good thoughts and intentions, helped by certain spiritual practices, that lead to good karma. At death, the individual is reborn as a different person, without memory of the previous life and without maintaining the relationships from the previous life. The journey to gain knowledge and to let go of self is repeated all over again. Eventually, after many, many lifetimes, one is released from this cycle of death and rebirth and is reunited to the impersonal Brahman.

Christians see our life's journey in much different terms. We believe that God created a world that was good and beautiful. God created humanity to live in love and fellowship with God and with one another. But, just as God gave us the freedom to think and act in ways that are good and loving, we also have freedom to act in selfish ways, giving in to greed, lust, pride, indifference, and violence.

In the sanctuary of the Church of the Resurrection we have a large stained-glass window—a mural telling the biblical story from Genesis 1 to Revelation 22. The window begins with the garden of Eden, and Adam and Eve plucking the fruit of the Tree of the Knowledge of Good and Evil—fruit God had forbidden them from eating. The scene is not intended to tell us about ancient history, but about ourselves. We are all Adam and Eve, turning away from God's will at times, listening to the voice of the serpent as they did, and after we've done what we knew we should not do, or failed to do what we knew we should do, paradise is lost. We find ourselves ashamed, or alienated from God and others. Christians don't see this as a result of ignorance, but sin. The word *sin*, in the Greek of the New Testament, is *hamartia*, which means "to miss the mark." Sin is missing the target or mark, and we all do this.

We see evidence of humanity's struggle with sin every day in our world. We see it on the news. We hear it in the ways we talk about other human beings. We see it in the wars that never seem to end. We see it in our own infidelity, in our struggles to do the right thing, in our failures to treat people with kindness, compassion, and mercy. We see it in the thousands of people who die every day from starvation and malnutrition-related diseases.

Salvation comes to us, according to the New Testament, not as a result of hundreds of reincarnations and after hundreds or thousands of years of gaining spiritual insights. We can't save ourselves through more spiritual knowledge. We can't perform enough good works to release us and reunite us to God. We cannot save ourselves. Instead, we need to be saved *from* ourselves. Our hearts have to be changed—we need conversion and new birth, and this is not something we can do on our own. It is something God does for us.

In Christianity, thankfully, we don't get what we deserve based on our works. It's not good karma that eventually saves us. It is, instead, the grace of God that saves us.

Christ came to reveal God to us, to heal us and to heal our world. He saves us. His life, death, and resurrection are the keys to that salvation. Christians believe that in yielding our lives to him, and through the Holy Spirit, we are changed and given the capacity to live our faith in a way that brings healing to us and to the world.

You see this emphasis in the Scripture passage at the beginning of this chapter from Paul's Letter to the Ephesians. Even though we were dead in our sins, Paul writes, God made us alive through Christ. It is not our own doing, nor is it the result of good works; it is God's gift. When we accept this gift through faith, God re-creates us in Christ Jesus to pass along the gift through love and good works. Christ working in us and through us transforms us into new people. Paul concludes, "We are God's accomplishment" (Ephesians 2:10). The original Greek for accomplishment is *poema*; we are God's "poetry."

Walking with a Personal God

While the Church of the Resurrection stained-glass window begins with Adam and Eve eating the forbidden fruit and paradise is lost, the window—reflecting the Christian Scriptures—ends with a picture of paradise restored. Revelation 22, the last chapter of the Christian Scriptures, ends in a garden, just as Genesis 1 began in a garden. Revelation paints a picture of a place and time where there will be no more suffering, sorrow, or pain. God will wipe away every tear from our eyes. This is a picture of our ultimate destiny according to the Bible. It is not dying and being reborn a thousand times until we are finally released from suffering and reunited to God like a drop of water to the ocean. Instead it is, at our death, joining Christ and the saints that have gone before us, into a realm where sorrow, pain, sin, and death have been banished.

I'm reminded of the words of Jesus on the night before his death, "My Father's house has room to spare. If that weren't the case, would I have told you that I'm going to prepare a place for you? When I go to prepare a place for you, I will return and take you to be with me so that where I am you will be too" (John 14:2-3). I love this picture of what happens at death—Jesus calls us by name and invites us to join him in the realm of endless light, joy, and peace—paradise.

Learning from Each Other

In faithful, committed Hindus I have met, I've seen a deep desire to know God and to do God's work and will. I've seen a deep sense of duty to love their neighbors as they love themselves. We share together a sense of the mystery and glory of God and the call to live a life of love.

We are different, but we share important things in common, and we can learn from one another. It was Gandhi's study of Christianity that led to and reinforced the idea of nonviolent resistance. Gandhi was a lawyer trained under the British Empire. He saw how the Indian people were treated as second-class citizens by the British, and he longed to do something about it. He found his inspiration in the Sermon on the Mount. "Don't love only those who love you back; love your enemies." "If someone strikes you on the cheek, turn the other cheek." On his office wall there was only one image of a religious figure. It wasn't Krishna, or the Buddha; it was an image of Jesus. He turned to Jesus' teaching to understand what noninjury might look like as an agent of change. He understood that nonviolence could be an incredibly powerful force.

People would sometimes ask Gandhi, "You talk about Jesus all the time. Are you a Christian?" As Gandhi explained, he didn't believe all of the same things that Christians believed. But he considered himself a follower of Jesus, because Jesus helped him see how living a life of noninjury and sacrificial love could actually change the world.

In the United States, Gandhi's example of living the non-violent teachings of Jesus inspired a young Baptist preacher named Martin Luther King Jr. King saw in Gandhi's leadership a picture of "soul force." King, the Baptist pastor, learned the power of nonviolent love from the Hindu Gandhi, who himself learned it from Jesus! King became a better Christian by studying Gandhi. And Gandhi became a better Hindu by studying Jesus.

Maybe the same could be true of us as we listen to and love our Hindu neighbors. My hope is that we will be the kind of people who understand our faith well enough to have a real dialogue with those of other faiths—and that we will not feel threatened by their faith but will listen with kindness, compassion, and empathy. Along the way, we may find that we have become better Christians.

Timeline
Buddhism and Christianity*

Dates	Buddhism	Christianity
		Prophet Jeremiah (626-587 BC)
600 BC		Prophet Ezekiel (593-571 BC)
	Siddhartha Gautama is born (563 BC)	Jerusalem and the Temple destroyed by the Babylonians (587 BC)
	Siddhartha leaves home to become a monk at age 29 (534 BC)	Babylonian Exile (586-539 BC)
		Jews return from Exile (539 BC)
	Siddhartha attains enlightenment and becomes the Buddha (528 BC)	Temple is rebuilt (520-515 BC)
500 BC	Siddhartha Gautama dies (483 BC)	Ezra and Nehemiah (ca. 450-400 BC)
400 BC		
300 BC		
200 BC		
100 BC	Pali Canon committed to writing (1st century BC)	Life of Jesus (4 BC-AD 29)
0		

*Dates for Buddhism based on the traditional date of 483 BC for the Buddha's death. An alternative scholarly view dates the Buddha's death to around 400 BC.

3.
BUDDHISM

I believe that the present suffering is nothing compared to the coming glory that is going to be revealed to us. . . .

We know that God works all things together for good for the ones who love God, for those who are called according to his purpose.

(Romans 8:18, 28)

Don't be anxious about anything; rather, bring up all of your requests to God in your prayers and petitions, along with giving thanks. Then the peace of God that exceeds all understanding will keep your hearts and your minds safe in Christ Jesus.

(Philippians 4:6-7)

Our study of Buddhism begins with a question: is Buddhism a religion or a philosophy? The answer is not as simple as you might think. As we'll see later in this chapter, the Buddha himself was agnostic when it came to the question of God. He saw what he was offering as a path for ending the experience of suffering, a path that did not depend upon faith in God. The path is not attempting to draw people close to any god. It does not purport to teach the will of any god. There are some Christians, Jews, and others who accept some of the philosophical ideas of Buddhism and appreciate its disciplines, while practicing their own faith.

Yet even as it remains agnostic about God and is seen by many of its adherents as a philosophy, it makes what seem to non-Buddhists to be religious claims about the nature of reality, and it teaches practices that are not dissimilar to the spiritual disciplines taught by other faiths. To me, Buddhism seems both a religion and a philosophy.

As with each of the faiths we'll consider, beliefs and practices vary widely among the world's 320 million Buddhists. And the Buddha's teaching is subject to differing interpretations, as are the teachings of those who followed him. There are several major schools, what we might call denominations, within Buddhism. Among the schools with the greatest number of adherents are Theraveda, Mahayana, and Vajrayana, but within each of these are also numerous subsects like Zen Buddhism.

This chapter offers a very broad overview of Buddhism that I hope will prove useful as we continue to seek answers to the questions that Christians ask about other religions. Though I have spent many hours reading about Buddhism, studying it in seminary, interviewing Buddhist leaders, and attending services at Buddhist centers, I write as a Christian, and my understanding is that of an outsider seeking to understand. I hope you will see this chapter as a primer, preparing you to do additional study on your own. With that in mind, let's begin our study of Buddhism.

The Story of the Buddha

The story of Buddhism starts with a man named Siddhartha Gautama, the man who became better known to history, after his own spiritual struggle, as the Buddha. We cannot be precise about the dates of his life. Traditionally, scholars believe he was born in 563 BC, though many today put the date of his birth around 480 BC. Whenever it was, we know that he was born in Lumbini, in what is today Nepal, on the southern side of the Himalayas. We also know that he died of food poisoning, at the age of eighty, in a place called Kushinagar, not far from the village where he was born.

Siddhartha's father was a prince, a wealthy tribal chief, who ruled a small kingdom. His mother died in childbirth. Consequently, his father did everything he could to protect young Siddhartha (I'll use his given name in telling that part of his story that occurred before his enlightenment) from every form of suffering as he grew up. He made sure the boy was always surrounded in his palace by beautiful things and beautiful people. Siddhartha wanted for nothing, and nothing threatened his world. He married at sixteen, a common age for marriage in that era, and he had a son. He continued to live in the lap of luxury for more than another decade. But by the time he was twenty-nine, Siddhartha was struggling, trying to understand who he was and his place in the world (much as many of us have done).

He told his father he wanted to leave the palace. He wanted to meet people beyond his own narrow, sheltered experience.

When Siddhartha grew up in Nepal, Hinduism was already a long-established religion on the Indian subcontinent. Buddhism began as a kind of reformation within Hinduism. This context is important to understanding what Siddhartha did and why. As you may recall from reading about Hinduism in the previous chapter, the supreme God was viewed as beyond all comprehension. Ordinary Hindus were taught that they had little direct access to God. They could approach God only through a member of the priestly caste, one of the Brahmins, who served as mediators with God. Siddhartha would not have had a personal faith in, or a direct experience of, God. What he knew of God from the Hinduism of his day was of little or no help in resolving his questions and struggles. So, Siddhartha asked his father for permission to see the world and to try to find answers to the questions with which he wrestled. His father allowed him to go.

Siddhartha left the palace with a chariot and a chariot driver in search of answers. The story that ensues, three journeys Siddhartha takes from the palace, is viewed by many Buddhists as historical but by others as apocryphal. Either way, the story is critical for understanding Buddhism.

Siddhartha and his charioteer hadn't gotten far before they came across a decrepit, very elderly man, bent from age. Siddhartha, who had been so carefully shielded from suffering, was deeply disturbed by seeing how the ravages of old age had affected the poor man. He asked his charioteer, "Is this the fate of all people?"

"Yes, Siddhartha," replied the charioteer. "All of us grow old."

Hearing this distressed Siddhartha's spirit so much that he returned to the palace.

Sometime later, Siddhartha had recovered his curiosity and his need for answers, and he wanted to venture out into the world again. In hopes of sparing his son from another disturbing sight, his father made sure there would be no old people along his route. Instead, Siddhartha and his driver encountered someone who was very ill, almost to the point of death. Again he asked the charioteer, "Is this the fate of all people?"

"Yes," his servant said. "All people will suffer illness at some point in their lives." And again, Siddhartha's spirit was so troubled that he went back to his "safe space" in the palace.

A few days later, Siddhartha ventured out one more time. His father prepared the way by making sure no elderly or sick people would cross their path. But he had not anticipated that, this time, Siddhartha and his charioteer would come across a funeral procession. The body of the deceased was laid out on a bier, in the Hindu manner. Siddhartha had never seen a dead body before. He asked his charioteer, "What is that?"

"Somebody who died," came the answer.

"Is this the fate of all people?"

"Yes," replied the charioteer. "One day, all of us will experience death."

The Burden of Reality

I think we can relate to the heartsick feeling Siddhartha experienced in what he saw on his trips beyond the palace. We learn at some point as children that we all grow old, get sick, and one day die. We've all known the anxiety, sadness, or grief he felt when faced with these universal dimensions of the human experience.

How do we live with the burden of this reality? How do we live knowing the world is transient, that nothing is permanent, and with a clear understanding that everyone will experience suffering? We try not to think about it too much, because it can be disturbing. But most of us come to these realizations gradually. We are able to work through these questions over time. Siddhartha was forced to confront them all at once, and he experienced an existential crisis.

Existentialists refer to Siddhartha's feelings, which are nearly universal among humans, as *angst*. The ancient Greek word from which it is derived, which is also the root of the word *anxiety*, means to strangle or to be unable to breathe. You've likely felt this kind of anxiety in your own life—and if you haven't yet, you will. Siddhartha refers to this as *dukha*, a word often translated as "suffering."

When Siddhartha had returned to the palace, his father saw his anxiety and sought to help his son. He threw a huge party to chase away his son's despair. But nothing helped. Siddhartha already had enjoyed everything of a material nature that a person could want. In fact, the inability of material pleasure to reduce his angst only served to increase his despair.

If material possessions could not take away suffering, thought Siddhartha, he would take the opposite approach. He decided to renounce the life of wealth and power forever. So one night when his wife and son were asleep, he left the palace. He entered a monastery and, as a traveling monk, pursued a life of extreme asceticism. He fasted and denied himself, at one point seeking to live on one grain of rice a day. We are so accustomed to seeing Buddha portrayed as large and laughing, but this is not what he looked like at this point in his life. He was on the verge of starvation. At some point, Siddhartha realized that self-denial had been no more effective than the pursuit of pleasure at relieving his angst.

The Awakening

At the age of thirty-five, after six years as a traveling monk, he had a profound, life-changing revelation. He sat down under a tree, known as the Bodhi Tree, and meditated, determined not to get up until he had found the key to living without anxiety, putting an end to this inner turmoil or suffering. For forty-nine days he sat under the tree, until he fell into a deep trance. In this trance state he came to see the world in a way he had never seen it before. When he awoke, he believed he understood the source of suffering and the path to overcoming it. He had attained enlightenment. In Pali (the language in which Buddhist scriptures were written in the first century BC), the word for "enlightened" is *budh*. Siddhartha Gautama had become the Buddha—the enlightened one.

The Buddha would spend the next forty-five years of his life teaching others about his insight and experience. He taught them a philosophical and meditative system that was meant to liberate human beings. He did not claim to be a god, nor did his disciples consider him one; instead, he was a teacher who set himself to the task of helping others be free from suffering. After he died, many followers carried forward his teachings, ultimately giving rise to the various schools of Buddhism we see today, and more broadly, to the Buddhist religion or philosophy.

The Buddha's teachings were passed down orally after his death, and they were not generally put in written form until shortly before the time of Jesus. The written summary of Buddhist teachings is called the Pali Canon, and within those writings is a collection of short wisdom sayings called the Dhammapada. Often, American students are assigned to read the Dhammapada in college.

Here's an example of the Buddha's teaching in the Dhammapada: "Hatred is never appeased by hatred in this world. By non-hatred alone is hatred appeased. This is a law eternal" (Dhammapada 1:5). That sounds much like something Martin Luther King Jr. said nearly twenty-five hundred years later: "Hate cannot drive out hate; only love can do that."

There are many parallels between the Dhammapada and the things we find in Scripture, particularly the Book of Proverbs.

Essential Buddhist Teachings

What was it that Siddhartha learned during his revelation that alleviated his sense of angst? What did he seek to teach others? We have space only to consider briefly a few of the most important tenets.

The insights that came to the Buddha as he sat under the Bodhi Tree, the essential path of Buddhism, are called the Four Noble Truths:

1. **Suffering is an integral part of life.** We all experience what the Buddha described as *dukha*: feelings of anxiety, pain, grief, and loss. Life is filled with anxiety and stress.

2. **Suffering results from attachments and desires.** Suffering, Buddhists believe, is the result of our clinging and attachments. We tend to cling to others, to possessions, to life itself.

3. **We can overcome suffering by overcoming our attachments.** When we are no longer attached to, or no longer cling to, things or people, suffering ceases.

4. **Following the Holy Eightfold Path is the way to find release from suffering.** The Holy Eightfold Path, also called the Noble Eightfold Path, is eight practices that lead to the extinguishing of attachment or craving, ultimately resulting in enlightenment. The path is often portrayed as a wheel with eight spokes.

The eight practices that form the Holy Eightfold Path are: (1) right (or wise) understanding, (2) right (or wise) thought,

(3) right speech, (4) right action, (5) right livelihood, (6) right effort, (7) right mindfulness, and (8) right concentration. I found it interesting as I sat with Buddhist teacher Venerable Urgyen Pete Machik Potts, that she summarized the Eightfold Path by noting that this entailed avoiding doing evil, doing all the good one can, and purifying one's mind. (If that sounds familiar to United Methodists, it should. The three "general rules" set down in the eighteenth century by John Wesley, founder of the Methodist movement, are often summarized as avoiding doing evil, doing good of every possible sort, and pursuing the practices that help one grow in the love of God.)

Buddhism vs. Hinduism

As I noted earlier, Buddhism began as something of a reform movement within Hinduism. Hinduism was the dominant religion in the region where the Buddha lived. Hindus today consider the Buddha a part of their tradition. And it is understandable that, just as Protestant Christianity shares so many essential beliefs with Roman Catholicism and Eastern Orthodox Christianity, Buddhism retained some of the elements of Hinduism.

For example, Buddhism and Hinduism both teach reincarnation. Both Hindus and Buddhists describe the nearly endless cycle of death and rebirth as *samsara*—a word that connotes a wandering journey in Hinduism and the cycle of suffering associated with death and rebirth in Buddhism. The Buddha himself was said to remember more than five hundred previous lives, both animal and human. (As a side note, it is interesting to me that I've met Christians who find the idea of reincarnation appealing, but in Buddhism and Hinduism it is something to be escaped.)

Buddhism also embraces the Hindu concept of *karma*—that our good and bad deeds determine the state we will occupy in the life to come.

But Buddhism also departs from Hinduism in significant ways.

For one thing, Buddhism is nontheistic. (Buddhism is the only major religion that does not center on a supreme God.) As noted earlier, the Buddha simply said that the question of God's existence is irrelevant for ending human suffering. Based on his experiences, his conclusion is understandable. He turned to the Hindu religious deities of his time and found no help with his *angst*.

As you'll recall from the previous chapter, Hindus believe in one supreme God, but they also believe that God is largely impersonal. The idea of having an individual relationship with God, of being able to receive a sense of peace from one's connection with God or answers to prayer from God, is alien to Hindus. In addition, in Hinduism the priestly caste are the intermediaries between everyone else and God. For Buddha, a member of the Warrior caste, the only way to approach God was to go make offerings to a priest, who then made offerings to the gods. There was no direct channel for Siddhartha Gautama to call upon the supreme God of Hinduism for help during his years of angst. It is understandable, based upon the Hinduism of his day, that the Buddha taught that God had no direct involvement in one's life and that one could believe in God, or not believe in God, and still accept the Four Noble Truths, live according to the Eightfold Path, and ultimately find release from *samsara*.

Being nontheistic does not mean that Buddhists are atheists. While there are Buddhists who are atheists, there are others who believe in a Supreme Being. Buddhists don't worship the Buddha (he himself did not wish to be worshiped) though they do revere him. They look to Buddha as a guide and example, hoping to achieve the kind of enlightenment that he achieved.

Buddhism also rejects the Hindu idea of a soul. You'll remember that, in Hinduism, the soul is the *atman*, a part of God that longs for reunification with God. The Buddha taught the concept of *anatman*, meaning "no soul." For Buddhists, there is no "I." Individual identity is merely an illusion. But if there is no self, no soul, then what is reborn in the cycle of death and rebirth? Here there is some debate within Buddhism. Some are content to consider it a paradox. I've read many Buddhist teachers attempt to explain how they reconcile the *anatman*— the belief that there is no soul, no self—with the idea that something of one's essence is reborn again and again (such that the Buddha could remember hundreds of previous lives). It is still unclear to me. What does seem clear to me is that, unlike many atheists who believe that there is nothing more after death—that in every way you cease to exist when your brain activity ceases—Buddhists believe that something is reborn in another life form. Some call this "something" your life energy.

For Buddhists, the end of this cycle of death and rebirth comes when you finally release all sense of otherness, all clinging and craving, and you become completely free from the cycle of death and rebirth. This state is called *nirvana* by both Buddhists and Hindus. But there is an important difference in how they see this state. Hinduism teaches that *nirvana* is the reunion of one's soul with God, like a drop of water being absorbed into a vast ocean. In Buddhism, which denies the existence of an individual soul, there is no reunification with a supreme God that may or may not exist. Instead, as one Buddhist lama explained it to me, upon achieving *nirvana*, the karmic energy that makes up a person's life force is extinguished, like

61

the light of a candle being blown out. Remember, however, that there are many different interpretations of Buddhism and not all Buddhists share this view. Venerable Urgyen Pete Machik Potts described nirvana not as being extinguished but as finally being released into the universe and absorbed with all other energy.

Differences Between Christianity and Buddhism

Christians and Buddhists can certainly find many things on which we would agree, and those things are well worth affirming. Many of the Buddha's words and teachings about the noble path, and the suffering that comes from clinging, are not dissimilar to things taught in the Bible. Some of it mirrors things taught by Jesus himself.

In a time when so many of us are living our lives at a frenetic pace, Christians can admire the Buddha's emphasis on meditative practices. In our ultra-materialistic society, we can agree with—and learn from—his teachings about not being attached to the things of this world. We also share much in common as it relates to ethical living.

I wish that space allowed us to explore all of the many points at which Buddhism and the Christian faith connect. I find much I appreciate within the Buddha's teaching. However, there are also many places where Buddhism and the Christian faith offer very different answers to the same questions and problems related to human existence and ultimate reality. Examining those differences may lead us to a better understanding of our own faith.

The Origin of and Solution to Suffering

Buddhism, as you read earlier in this chapter, grew out of one man's search for answers to the problem of human suffering.

Christians do not deny the reality of suffering. In fact, most of us have experienced the kind of angst that led Siddhartha Gautama on his quest to find peace.

From the Buddhist perspective, the problem of suffering lies with us. We attach ourselves to material needs and to things that are impermanent. We cling and want to hold on to people and things in a fundamentally impermanent world. The illusion of self is part of what makes this suffering possible.

Christians would agree that clinging or attachment may cause suffering. I think of what were traditionally called the seven deadly sins: lust, gluttony, greed, indifference, anger, envy, and pride. In a sense, every one of them is about clinging, attachment, or inappropriate desire and each can produce angst, fear, and sadness in ourselves and lead to harm to others.

I remember speaking with a woman who desperately wanted a job that would have represented a big promotion. Her entire sense of self-worth was tied to getting that job. When it did not happen, she was devastated. Her desire, her attachment to something impermanent, caused her to suffer. She could have learned from the Buddha's teaching.

But while it might seem like mere semantics, for Christians the largest cause of suffering isn't clinging, attachment, or desire. It's sin. And while clinging or attachment can be sin, sin within the Christian faith has a broader definition.

The Greek word for sin used in the New Testament is *hamartia*, which means to miss the mark or stray from the path. In Christianity (as in Judaism and even Buddhism), there is a right path. For Christians and Jews, that path represents God's will for humanity. When we stray from that path, we suffer and often other people suffer as well. The right path involves practicing justice and loving-kindness. When we stray from this path, when we act in unjust or unloving ways, we bring pain. Infidelity in marriage, cruelty toward others, an unwillingness to help those in need are all examples of straying from the right path resulting in pain to others and often to ourselves.

Attachment to unhealthy and selfish desires can certainly contribute to these varying manifestations of suffering. Over and over, Jesus cautioned against putting too much value in transitory, material things. He told us to focus on treasure in heaven rather than impermanent treasures on earth. In the Sermon on the Mount, Jesus taught us not to worry about what we will eat tomorrow or what we will wear. He said to seek first the kingdom of God and God's righteousness, and everything else would take care of itself.

But Christians also recognize that some attachments are from God. We are meant to be attached to friends and family, to spouses and children, to our neighbors—these are not unhealthy attachments, but instances of covenant love.

At times we experience sorrow because we love deeply. I think of the many times I've broken down and wept as I tried to communicate to my daughters just how deeply I love them. That kind of sorrow is an expression of a much deeper love. But one senses that the Buddha would consider it to be clinging or an unhealthy attachment and my tears an expression of suffering.

For Christians, the answer to suffering is not to detach ourselves from all people, places, and things. Jesus did not tell us to be detached; he told us to be attached first and foremost to God, and then all the other attachments in our life will fall into place.

Instead of calling people to detachment, Christianity calls us to repentance. In Greek, the word is *metanoia*, which means, literally, to think differently afterward. It is a change of thinking, a change of mind, that results in a change of heart and ultimately a change of behavior. Repentance is a kind of awakening or enlightenment. It's the enlightenment the prodigal son experienced at the lowest point in his life, when he realized it was time to turn around and ask for his father's forgiveness. *Metanoia* occurs when we realize that we have injured other people (and ourselves) or turned against God as we strayed from the path that God set out for us to follow. We want to bring an end to that pain, so we confess and try to make amends with God or the person we've injured. The change in our behavior opens the door to reconciliation and a changed relationship. It takes away the suffering that we've been inflicting upon one another. It helps bring healing to the world.

God or No God? Personal or Impersonal?

There are other kinds of suffering aside from the harm we do to one another from missing the mark. These kinds of suffering are bound to the human condition, and they include the infirmity of old age, sickness, and death that led to Siddhartha's quest for enlightenment. The Buddha's answer was detachment from clinging.

But Christianity has a different answer, and it flows from our belief in a personal relationship with a God who is anything but detached from our lives. We believe that, through the person of Jesus, we see a God who loves and cares for humanity. In Jesus we see a God who weeps over those who are suffering, a God who is moved to compassion when he sees the sick, broken, or hurting. We see in the Christian faith a God who searches for lost sheep in order to bring them back to the right path.

Through his own suffering, death, and resurrection, Jesus also taught us about what is impermanent and what is permanent. He showed us that God's undying love has the final word over human violence, human pain, and human death. Jesus taught that, through him, we can find abundant life here and now and in the resurrection in the life to come.

65

Christians do not believe that, in God, we will find an end to all suffering in this life. At the center of Christian faith is Jesus, who was tortured to death on a cross. He did not promise that in following him we'd eliminate suffering. In fact, he promised that by following him we would experience trouble and be called upon to "take up your cross." Jesus' answer to suffering is a promise that suffering will never have the final word. This is the powerful message of Easter—that suffering and sickness, sin and death will never have the final word.

Because of his experience with a personal God, Paul could write to the Philippians the verses at the beginning of this chapter, verses that describe the inner peace and surpassing joy he felt amid his own hardships as he sat imprisoned: "Don't be anxious about anything; rather, bring up all of your requests to God in your prayers and petitions, along with giving thanks. Then the peace of God that exceeds all understanding will keep your hearts and minds safe in Christ Jesus" (Philippians 4:6-7).

Suffering: To Be Avoided or Embraced?

I would add one other point about suffering: the Christian Scriptures teach us that suffering is not always bad. (And though he sought an end to suffering, I would venture a guess that the Buddha might agree some suffering is redemptive.) To be sure, suffering is often bad, a result of sin or inappropriate clinging. But sometimes suffering is an expression of love, a part of loving. Placed in God's hands, suffering is almost always redemptive. So the Apostle Paul could write, "suffering produces endurance, and endurance produces character, and character produces hope, and hope does not disappoint us, because God's love has been poured into our hearts through the Holy Spirit that has been given to us" (Romans 5:3b-5 NRSV).

The Bible speaks of a kind of love demonstrated by Jesus as he gave himself for us. The Greek word used to describe this love in the New Testament is *agape*, and it is often seen as a selfless and sacrificial love that might make one vulnerable to suffering. There is no greater love, Jesus told his disciples, than to lay down one's life for one's friends. Christ's suffering and death is itself a means of redemption and healing for the world.

God's Place in Our Lives

The point at which Buddhism and Christianity differ most fundamentally is the question of God. Whereas Buddhism says, "Maybe there is a God, maybe not, but it doesn't really matter," Christian faith is built on the assertion that there is a God, and that this God is not only the Creator of heaven and earth but also personal, near, and revealed to us in Jesus. Christian faith is a simple trust that no matter what happens in life, God walks with us, and therefore, even in the face of suffering, we find solace and hope.

Soul or No Soul? Extinction or Eternal Life?

Finally, the concept of an individual soul is a key difference between Buddhism and Christianity. Christians reject the idea that there is no soul, that our individual identity is just an illusion, and that our ultimate goal is to experience the release of the energy that animates us back into the universe.

Christianity insists that we have a soul, that there really is a *you*; it is not an illusion. Even though our physical body is transitory and ultimately dies, there is something more to you than your physical body. And when the body dies, we continue to live in a "new body" in a place spoken of in Scripture as heaven, paradise, and by other words. Regarding this the

67

Apostle Paul wrote, "We know that if the tent that we live in on earth is torn down, we have a building from God. It's a house that isn't handmade, which is eternal and located in heaven" (2 Corinthians 5:1).

I've been with hundreds of people as they approached death. Some were afraid, and I helped them trust in God and find peace. Others felt the sadness of saying goodbye to those they loved. Our tears and sadness as we approach death are not a sign that we are clinging, nor do we hope to reach a stage of detachment that we no longer weep when someone we love dies. Our tears are a sign of a deep love. We will suffer from this kind of grief or sadness for a time. But our faith in Christ and in Easter leads us to grieve as people who have hope.

I love how the New Testament ends, with the vision of John the Revelator of a new heaven and a new earth. In that place, John wrote, "He will wipe away every tear from their eyes. Death will be no more. There will be no mourning, crying, or pain anymore, for the former things have passed away" (Revelation 21:4). Christians believe that when our earthly life ends, we are not extinguished like a candle, nor are we reabsorbed into the cosmos after a cycle of death and reincarnation.

Appreciating Buddhism

Despite our differences, there is much I appreciate and love in Buddhism: I love Siddhartha's story of angst that led him on his quest. I can relate to this. I value a number of the Buddha's wise sayings. I think his emphasis on refraining from evil, doing good, and purifying one's heart is closely aligned with spiritual practices in the Christian faith. And I value Buddhism's emphasis on meditation—on quieting one's heart and anxieties.

Among the things that made me a better Christian after studying Buddhism was something that is not unique to Buddhism, but is highlighted in Buddhism: the idea of mindfulness. In Buddhism this is often practiced in conjunction with meditation. I think this has great value for anyone. But the mindfulness that stuck with me was more about paying attention.

I think we often live our lives failing to see what is happening around us. We fail to pay attention. But it is in paying attention, being truly awake, listening and noticing people and experiences, that we find the greatest sense of being fully alive

Recently I had a meeting with several of our staff just outside of the sanctuary at the Church of the Resurrection. It was a cold and snowy winter's day and there were few people in the building apart from a sparse office staff.

As we were meeting, out of the corner of my eye I saw a woman walking out of our sanctuary. I wondered why she was there on a day when everyone else was gone. But I didn't dwell on that thought and started to turn back to join the conversation with our staff. But something told me I needed to go check on her. I left my meeting, and as I drew closer I could tell she had been crying.

As I spoke to her, I learned that she had been sitting in the sanctuary, praying and weeping. She told me of the various ways in which it felt like her life was coming apart at the seams. She hadn't known where else to turn, so she'd come to the church. I listened to her story, then asked if I could pray with her. I didn't solve her problems. But in that moment, I sought to embody God's love and care for her. That evening, I received a note, a message sent via Facebook, that said, "Pastor Adam, today you were the presence of God for me as I felt so very hopeless. Thank you for noticing me and stepping away from your meeting. It gave me hope."

At that moment, this woman's need was far more important than my staff meeting, yet I almost missed it. These kinds of experiences happen all the time when we are paying attention. Each morning I slip out of bed and to my knees to say my morning prayers. Among my daily prayers are some variation of these words, "Help me to pay attention today, Lord. Lead me, guide me, and use me to bless others." When you're mindful, when you pay attention to the nudge of the Spirit, you are likely to find yourself being used by God to care for others or do some other meaningful work. I'm reminded of the famous saying, "Life is what happens to you while you're busy making other plans." It is often in the interruptions that we find the most meaningful part of our day. This idea of paying attention is one of the things I appreciate about Buddhism.

As one last example, I recently completed one of the health screenings that Church of the Resurrection makes available for its employees. During my screening, a young woman pricked my finger to get a blood sample to measure my cholesterol. She took my blood pressure and made me stand on the scales to measure my weight. While this was going on, we were having a conversation, mostly just small talk at first. But somehow we began talking about fear. I mentioned that I had just finished writing a book about fear, and she said, "I'd really like to read that book," which suggested to me that she had been wrestling with fear at some point. So we began to talk about that.

I mentioned that one of the things that helps me with fear is my faith, and I asked if she was involved in a church. She told me that she and her husband were new to the community, that they had two small children, and that they were an interfaith couple who were struggling to find a community of faith. She was Jewish, her husband was Christian. They wanted to find a community that would welcome them both. I told her that I was in the midst of a sermon series on various religions and that the next weekend's sermon was on Judaism. I invited her to join us.

And then she said, "Do you ever feel like you have conversations you were meant to have?"

I told her, "All the time."

There are significant places where Christians and Buddhists disagree. But there are also places where we share common ground. It was in studying Buddhism years ago that I was inspired to be much more intentional about paying attention, and that made me a better Christian.

Timeline
Judaism and Christianity*

Dates	Judaism	Christianity
0	Death of King Herod the Great (4 BC)	Life of Jesus (4 BC-AD 29)
		Paul's missionary journeys and letters (AD 45-65)
	Destruction of the Temple (AD 70)	Gospels committed to writing (AD 70-100)
	Development of oral law (pre-539 BC -AD 200)	
AD 100	Mishnah is written and codified (ca. AD 70-200)	
AD 200		
AD 300		Council of Nicea (AD 325)
	Jerusalem Talmud (ca. AD 350-400)	General Agreement on NT canon (ca. AD 350-382)
AD 400		Council of Chalcedon (AD 451)
AD 500	Babylonian Talmud (ca. AD 500)	

*Because Judaism and Christianity share the same history up to the time of Jesus, this timeline will focus on the development of Judaism and Christianity in the centuries following Jesus.

4.

JUDAISM

One of the legal experts heard their dispute and saw how well Jesus answered them. He came over and asked him, "Which commandment is the most important of all?"

Jesus replied, "The most important one is Israel, listen! Our God is the one Lord, and you must love the Lord your God with all your heart, with all your being, with all your mind, and with all your strength. *The second is this,* You will love your neighbor as yourself. *No other commandment is greater than these."*

(Mark 12:28-31)

In January of each year, the world observes International Holocaust Remembrance Day on the anniversary of the liberation of Auschwitz-Birkenau, January 27, 1945. It was that same week, in 1933, that Adolf Hitler assumed power as Germany's chancellor. He brought with him a philosophy that white Europeans of Nordic descent were the "master race"

73

(or, in German, *herrenvolk*). Other races—people of color, Slavic peoples—were inferior. They were *untermenschen*— literally, "lower people" or subhumans. There was actually a scale according to which the Nazis rated those they deemed *untermenschen* based on their physical appearance and genetic background.

On this Nazi scale of human worth, those at the very bottom, the lowest of the "lower people," were those of Semitic origin: Jews. In addition, Nazi propaganda began to blame Jews for Germany's defeat in World War I as well as for the harsh economic conditions in the aftermath of that war.

Thus began the Nazis' gradual campaign, first to dehumanize Jews, then to foster disdain for the Jews, then to justify discrimination against them, and, ultimately, to eliminate the Jewish population. Hitler's "final solution" resulted in the slaughter of six million European Jews, who represented more than one-third of the Jewish population of the world.

At the time, 99 percent of the German population claimed to be Christian. How could Christians come to accept the step-by-step persecution, then slaughter, of the Jewish people?

At first, many Germans refused to believe that the Nazis' anti-Jewish rhetoric could lead to such a barbaric conclusion. They had friends who were Jewish; they had Jewish doctors or bankers or lawyers. They knew that German Jews had faithfully served the Fatherland in the Great War; how could anyone now say that these people were somehow undermining the nation?

But gradually, the steady drip of anti-Semitic rhetoric began to seep into the subconscious of many of the German people. When people in authority say something enough times, regardless of how absurd or grotesque the claim may be, the idea begins to take root in the minds of many, particularly when the rhetoric plays upon people's fears. Others believed these ideas were wrong, but many were afraid to speak up. Thus the Nazi propaganda machine prepared the way for the first restrictions of civil rights for Jews beginning in 1933. By 1935, German Jews were stripped of their citizenship. In November 1938, on the "night of broken glass" the Nazi paramilitary and German civilians damaged and looted seven thousand Jewish shops and damaged fourteen hundred synagogues, in hundreds of cases destroying them. In the aftermath, thirty thousand German Jews were arrested and taken to concentration camps. There were some non-Jews who protested these events, some heroically standing against them. But many more were silent, while others actively supported the destruction of Jewish property and the imprisonment of Jewish people. These events ultimately led to the mass incarceration and murder of millions of Jews.

How could Christians who believe in the command to "love thy neighbor" tolerate this genocide against their neighbors? How could they, as followers of the Jewish Messiah, let themselves believe that Jews were an evil influence that must be eliminated? How could one of the most cultured nations in Europe descend into such collective barbarism?

The painful truth is that vicious and violent anti-Semitism was a phenomenon that occurred time and again in Christian Europe. In Spain, Jews were treated so oppressively by their Christian rulers that they welcomed the Muslim invaders from North Africa in the eighth century. In 1290, King Edward I issued a royal edict expelling Jews from England. When the Black Plague swept across Europe in the 1300s, Jews were often blamed for the plague, and many were killed. In 1492, the year that Columbus sailed west across the Atlantic, King Ferdinand and Queen Isabella of Spain ordered all Jews in the land to convert to Christianity, leave, or face death. In the late 1800s, waves of Russian and Polish Jews emigrated to North and

South America to escape the terrorizing pogroms of the Russian tsars, whose secret police spread a myth that Jews murdered Christian children and drank their blood at Passover. Sadly, most of the history of Christians and Jews over the span of two thousand years has been marked by such episodes of prejudice and persecution.

There was no Holocaust in America, but anti-Semitism was very much alive here. It just took a different and less obscene form. Here's an example that hits close to home for me. After World War II ended, as soldiers were coming home and the Great Depression was over, there was a massive wave of homebuilding across the country. But even as Americans were seeing images of Jews in concentration camps, these new subdivisions that were springing up were imposing covenants and restrictions to keep Jews out of the neighborhoods. I found one such covenant from a neighborhood near our church that forbade ownership by "any person who is more than one-fourth of the Semitic race."[1] This kind of formal anti-Semitism persisted until the 1990s. It was not until 1991 that one of the oldest and most prestigious country clubs in Kansas City finally allowed its first Jewish family to join.

While such overt prejudice is no longer accepted publicly, anti-Semitism has not disappeared. Our congregation experienced one such act on Palm Sunday of 2014. You might have read about it. A man known for his anti-Semitic rants drove to the Jewish Community Center in Kansas City, determined, he said, to kill Jews. He killed two people there, and a third person at a Jewish retirement community a few blocks away. He thought he was killing Jews; instead he killed two members of my congregation, and a devout Catholic. After his arrest, the man was shouting "Heil Hitler!" from the back seat of the police car.

More recently we've seen the alt-right emboldened and marching in places like Charlottesville, Virginia, carrying torches and shouting, "Jews will not replace us!" and spewing other anti-Jewish rhetoric. This kind of hatred is on the increase. According to the Anti-Defamation League, there was a 57 percent jump in anti-Semitic incidents in the United States in 2017.[2]

Most Christians in this country condemned the marches as un-Christian—a terrible perversion of what it means to be human. But throughout the history of our faith, the poisonous seeds of anti-Semitism took root among many who claimed to be Christians. Those seeds were watered and cultivated by misunderstanding and bad theology. Anti-Semitism reflects one of the tragic sins of the church over the centuries. One wonders how the founders of the Christian faith would view anti-Semitism given Jesus, his disciples, the Apostle Paul, and most of the earliest Christians were Jews.

Anti-Semitism is a perversion of the Christian faith's values. It is this kind of hate, born of fear and misunderstanding, that is a major reason I wrote this book and why I'm grateful you are reading it. My hope is that as we study the other faiths and grow in our understanding, we will see our neighbors of other faiths as our fellow human beings, and that knowing them better will help us better love our neighbors as we love ourselves.

Biblical History of Judaism

The Hebrew Bible (Christians refer to it as the "Old Testament" but for our Jewish friends, it is simply the Bible) begins with the story of Creation. It actually starts with two different versions of the Creation story. The first is a poetic liturgy or creed asserting the goodness of God's creation. The second, written in prose, climaxes with Adam and Eve eating the forbidden fruit and being expelled from the garden of Eden. These dual emphases, the goodness of God from whom all blessings flow and the propensity for humans to turn away from God, run throughout the rest of the Hebrew Bible.

The stories that follow Creation in the first eleven chapters of Genesis include the Flood and the Tower of Babel. These, along with the Creation stories, have parallels in other ancient Near Eastern religions, though the Genesis stories are told differently and have very distinctive theological emphases.

After these initial stories, the biblical narrative focuses on a man named Abram and his wife, Sarai. Their story begins around 2000 BC (give or take a couple of hundred years) in the city of Ur, in modern-day Iraq. Soon, they move with Abram's father and nephew to the city of Haran in southeastern Turkey. One day, in Haran, God spoke to Abram, as recorded in Genesis 12: "Leave your land, your family, and your father's household for the land that I will show you. I will make of you a great nation and will bless you. I will make your name respected, and you will be a blessing. I will bless those who bless you, those who curse you I will curse; all the families of the earth will be blessed because of you" (Genesis 12:1-3). In the next verse, we read, "Abram left just as the Lord told him" (v. 4).

Abraham and Sarah (God changed their names slightly in Genesis 17), at the age of seventy-five and sixty-five, respectively, left Haran and traveled to the land of Canaan in modern-day Israel and Palestine, and settled there (with a brief sojourn in Egypt). They eventually had two sons. The first was Ishmael, by a surrogate mother, Sarah's maidservant Hagar. Muslims trace their faith to Abraham through Ishmael. The second, born to Sarah late in life, was given the name Isaac, through whom Jews trace their faith. Isaac and his wife, Rebekah, had two sons, Esau and Jacob. Jacob's name was changed to Israel (meaning "one who wrestles with God"), and from Genesis 25 on, the rest of the Hebrew Bible is the story of Israel's descendants.

Israel had twelve sons and one daughter. These sons become the ancestors of twelve clans, known as the twelve tribes of Israel. Because of a famine in the land of Canaan, these sons ended up migrating from Canaan to Egypt, and they settled in the Nile River Delta in a region called the land of Goshen. The Egyptians eventually enslaved the Israelites, who remained enslaved there for hundreds of years.

In the thirteenth century before Christ (or earlier, there is debate about the dating), God called an eighty-year-old sheepherder named Moses, once an adopted member of Pharaoh's household but at the time a fugitive from the law, to deliver the Israelites from slavery and to lead them back to the land of Canaan, the land originally promised to Abraham and Sarah and their descendants. With God's powerful help, Moses did in fact deliver the Israelites, leading them into the Sinai wilderness.

At Mount Sinai, God made a covenant with the people of Israel. He gave to Moses the terms of the covenant, a law code by which the people were to live in relationship with God, with one another, and with the nations around them. The essence of the Law was captured by Ten Commandments etched on stone tablets. Concerning this covenant or binding agreement God was making with God's people, God said, "If you faithfully obey me and stay true to my covenant, you will be my most precious possession out of all the peoples, since the whole earth belongs to me. You will be a kingdom of priests for me and a holy nation" (Exodus 19:5-6a).

Included in the books of Exodus, Leviticus, Numbers, and Deuteronomy is the story of the liberation of the Israelite slaves,

79

numerous laws reflecting the terms of God's covenant with Israel, and the journey from Egypt to the edge of the Promised Land.

The people eventually entered and conquered the land God promised to Abraham hundreds of years before. The rest of the Hebrew Bible tells the story of Israel's history from the conquest of Canaan to about the year 165 BC.* Included in this story are court histories of the various rulers of the descendants of Israel, poetry, proverbs, prayers and songs of the people, and writings attributed to Israel's prophets: social and religious critics who called the people to repentance and to practice justice, mercy, and righteousness.

Israel's story recorded in Scripture is the story of a people who were rescued by God, who entered into a covenant with God, yet who repeatedly abandon that covenant. As the people turned from God, the prophets would warn them that God would remove his protection from their little nation, resulting in their being attacked and ultimately conquered by neighboring empires. In 722 BC, the Assyrians attacked and destroyed the northern half of the Promised Land, forcing the Israelites living in the north to relocate to Assyria where most were eventually absorbed into the Assyrian Empire.

The southern half of what had been Israel, by then known as the Kingdom of Judah, after repeated warnings from its prophets, was conquered by the Babylonian Empire in 586 BC. Much of its population was forcibly relocated to Babylon. Unlike their northern neighbors, the people of Judah (the Jewish people) worked to retain and reclaim their national and religious

---

* Traditionally the period of the Hebrew Bible was said to end about 400 BC, but most mainline scholars date the Book of Daniel to around 165 BC and see it looking back to an earlier period in order to speak to the political and religious situation of this later period.

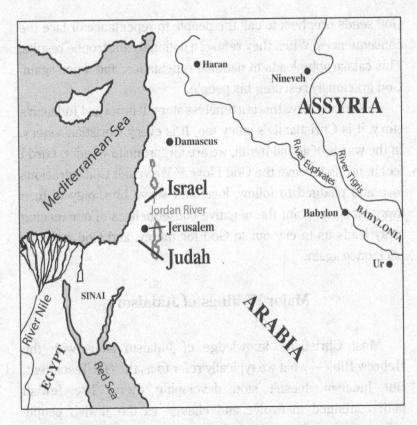

identity. They repented of their infidelity to God, and they were eventually delivered from the Babylonians and, in 539 BC, were allowed to return to their homeland.

The Jewish people, upon returning from exile, rebuilt their cities and the temple in Jerusalem. Even so, they would eventually struggle, once again, to be obedient to God. Thus, new prophets arose to call them to repentance, warning once more of the consequences of forsaking God's protection and care.

Throughout the Hebrew Bible, we find the following cycle repeated again and again. God graciously rescues his people from afflictions. In response, the people pledge fidelity to God. Yet, over time, the people inevitably wander away from God.

God sends prophets to call the people to repentance or face the consequences. When they refuse, a national catastrophe results. This catastrophe leads to national repentance, and, once again, God graciously rescuing his people.

In so many ways this is a timeless story. It is not just Judaism's story, it is Christianity's story too. It is every Christian's story. In the words of an old hymn, we are all "prone to wander, Lord I feel it, prone to leave the God I love."[3] We've felt God's gracious love and pledged to follow, love, and serve him, only to turn away. At some point the negative consequences of our turning away leads us to cry out to God for mercy, and God takes us back once again.

Major Writings of Judaism

Most Christians' knowledge of Judaism stops with the Hebrew Bible—what we typically refer to as the Old Testament. But Judaism doesn't stop developing there. The Jewish faith continued to evolve and change as the Jewish people reflected upon God and God's covenant in the light of their continued experiences and the changing world. This continued development of Judaism is reflected in Jewish religious writings that were composed after the Hebrew Bible or Old Testament period. Most Christians know very little about these works. Let's review the writings that make up the Hebrew Bible as well as those important bodies of writings that, while not a part of Judaism's Bible, are a part of its sacred traditions.

The Tanakh

The Tanakh is another word for the Hebrew Bible. The word is an acronym (TNK) drawn from combining the initial letters or sounds of the three collections of documents that make up the Tanakh: Torah, Nevi'im, and Ketuvim. The order in which these collections appear in the Hebrew Bible corresponds roughly to the time when they took shape.

Torah

Torah means "law" or "teachings" and specifically refers to the laws and teaching associated with Moses. These are the first five books of the Hebrew Bible. They recount God's covenant with Noah, Abraham, and Moses. They include the story of God's deliverance of the Israelites from captivity and the Law God gave to Moses and the Israelites as the terms of his covenant with them. These books are the most authoritative of the Scriptures within Judaism. The Ten Commandments are a distillation of the more than six hundred laws contained in the Torah. Two of the Laws in the Torah were identified by Jesus as the most important: love God with all of your being, and love your neighbor as you love yourself.

Nevi'im

Nevi'im means "prophets." In the Jewish Scriptures, the prophets include books that the Christian Old Testament places among the historical narratives: Joshua, Judges, First and Second Samuel, and First and Second Kings. For Jews these are counted among the prophets because they contain stories of what are referred to as the "former prophets," people like Samuel, Nathan, Elijah, Elisha, and others. The Nevi'im also includes the "latter prophets," books that contain the sayings or writings of Israel's prophets including Isaiah, Jeremiah, Ezekiel, and the other shorter prophetic books found in the prophetic section of the Christian Old Testament.

83

Ketuvim

Ketuvim means "writings." The Writings of the Hebrew Bible include Israel's wisdom literature and poetry—books like Psalms, Proverbs, and Job. They also include everything else in the Protestant Old Testament that is not included in the Law and the Prophets—books like 1 and 2 Chronicles (one book in the Hebrew Bible, not two), Ezra and Nehemiah (also one book in the Hebrew Bible), and many others.

Some sects in first-century Judaism recognized only the Torah as authoritative and sacred, seeing the other documents as part of the tradition of Judaism, but not Scripture (the Samaritans and the Sadducees viewed the writings in this way). Others saw the prophets and at least some of the writings as sharing in the authoritative status of the Torah. The Tanakh was the Bible of Jesus and the apostles (the New Testament was written decades after the death of Jesus). Jesus regularly quotes the Hebrew Bible from memory during his ministry, in his temptations, in times of prayer, and from the cross. He draws from all three sections of the Tanakh in his teaching and preaching. The books he most frequently quotes are Deuteronomy (the Law), Isaiah (the Prophets), and Psalms (the Writings).

The Talmud

Most of the documents that make up the Hebrew Bible took their final form in the period following the Jewish exile in Babylon. Following the Exile, Jews developed a vast body of oral law interpreting the Torah and applied it to everyday life. These laws were eventually written down, including some of the debates surrounding these laws, and codified around two hundred years after the birth of Christ. This body of work is called the Mishnah.

Rabbinical scholars went on to debate and write commentaries on the *Mishnah*. These commentaries were composed by Jewish communities in Tiberias and Caesarea in the Holy Land and by the Jewish community in Babylonia. The commentaries (including sermons) on the Mishnah are quite extensive. They are known as the *Gemara*. The Gemara is thousands of pages in length. The Gemara and the Mishnah together are known as the *Talmud*. There are two versions of the Talmud, corresponding to the two versions of the Gemara: the Babylonian Talmud and the Jerusalem Talmud.

Within Christianity there are things that function for Christians in a way similar to how the Talmud functions for Jews. Catholicism speaks of the church's "magisterium," the work of the bishops and popes to interpret and establish the teachings of the church. The writings of the early church, known collectively as the "church fathers," function as another body of writings that help Christians understand how the church of the first four hundred years of Christianity understood and interpreted the Scriptures and Christian theology. The creeds of the Christian church also serve to summarize the church's understanding of its theology as articulated by various councils of bishops held during the third, fourth, and fifth centuries.

Methodists and others speak of this ongoing interpretive work as the church's "tradition" and hold it as an important way in which the Holy Spirit helps us discern how we read, interpret, and apply Scripture.

Branches within Judaism

Judaism is not a monolithic faith, and while it traces its faith to Moses, modern Judaism has been shaped by its long, rich history to the present time. Just as there are denominations

85

within Christianity, there are branches or divisions within Judaism. In the United States, there are three major branches of Judaism (along with smaller branches within each of the major ones), falling on a spectrum of most conservative to most liberal or progressive. These are Orthodox, Conservative, and Reform (there are other groups, and subgroups, but these are the three largest streams of Judaism in the United States).

Orthodox Judaism

Orthodox Judaism is the most conservative stream within the Jewish religion. Orthodox Jews generally believe that the Torah was given by God to Moses on Mount Sinai, and as such the Torah represents the very words of God. Since the Law was given by God it carries a divine authority and is to be adhered to as closely as possible. The Mishnah, the oral law, is also thought to have been given by God, and hence both the Torah and the Mishnah are seen to express God's continuing will for the Jewish people. Orthodox Jews adhere strictly to Jewish laws, both those in the Torah and those found in the Mishnah.

Among Orthodox Jews are Modern Orthodox, who embrace elements of modern society and thought while seeking to live as closely as possible according to the precepts of the Torah. Many Orthodox, however, reject modernity. These include Haredi Jews, often referred to as "Ultra-Orthodox" by others, and within the Haredi tradition, the Hasidic Jews. Men tend to dress in black and wear beards and hats, while women dress in modest attire.

About 10 percent of American Jews are Orthodox.

Conservative Judaism

The designation "Conservative Judaism" (also sometimes called Positive Historical Judaism) can be a bit confusing for Christians, as Orthodox Judaism represents the most conservative of the Jewish traditions, and Conservative Judaism is actually what some would call "moderate." In many ways this movement in Judaism is similar to mainline Christianity, particularly the more moderate mainline denominations. "Conservative" here represents the attempt to conserve Judaism's traditions, while at the same time embracing reform. Conservative rabbis tend to embrace insights from modern biblical scholarship regarding the Torah and its development over centuries, written and edited by people who were inspired by God. The Mishnah is considered to be important human interpretations of the Torah, but not as something handed down by God.

There is a wide range of biblical interpretation among Conservative Jews, from more conservative to more progressive. Among the phrases that have defined this movement in Judaism is "tradition and change." In 1983, Conservative Judaism voted to allow the ordination of women. In 2006, Conservative Judaism allowed local congregations to set their own policy regarding same-sex marriage, and in 2012 formally allowed for the ordination of gay and lesbian people.

About 18 percent of American Jews are a part of a Conservative congregation.

Reform Judaism

Reform Judaism represents the most progressive or liberal form of Judaism. It embraces most enlightenment ideas and higher criticism's approach to studying Scripture, viewing the Torah as inspired by God but also shaped by its historical context. The ethical imperatives of Judaism, those addressing the call to pursue justice and loving-kindness, are retained within Reform Judaism, but keeping kosher and observance of much of the

Torah and Mishnah are not required. Within Reform Judaism there are more traditional and more progressive expressions. Reform Judaism places great emphasis on *tikkun olam*—repairing or healing the earth (more on this in a moment). Reform Jews also accept the ordination of women and gay and lesbian people.

About 35 percent of American Jews are within the Reform tradition, making it the largest branch of Judaism in America.

What Jews Believe

The Shema: The Lord is God, the Lord alone

To be a Jew is to believe in one God, as expressed by the central creed of Judaism, the Shema: "Hear, O Israel: The LORD is our God, the LORD alone. You shall love the LORD your God with all your heart, and with all your soul, and with all your might" (Deuteronomy 6:4-5 NRSV). Faithful Jews will recite the Shema every morning when they wake up, and again every night before they go to bed. They will hope that they have enough strength and presence of mind to make it their last words before they die.

In the passage from Mark's Gospel cited at the beginning of this chapter, we read:

> *One of the legal experts heard their dispute and saw how well Jesus answered them. He came over and asked him, "Which commandment is the most important of all?"*
>
> *Jesus replied, "The most important one is* Israel, listen! Our God is the one Lord, and you must love the Lord your God with all your heart, with all your being, with all your mind, and with all your strength."
>
> *(Mark 12:28-30)*

Jesus was a Jew who named the Shema as the most important of all commands.

The Golden Rule

Because the command to love God captures the essence of Judaism, in one sense the rest of the Law is a commentary on the Shema. What does it mean to love God with all your being? It means not worshiping other gods, for one thing. It means keeping the Sabbath holy. In particular, it means loving our neighbors, who, after all, are made in the image of God. As Mark's Gospel recounts, Jesus told the scribes that the other great commandment was to love your neighbor as you love yourself.

Rabbi Hillel, a revered Jewish leader at the time Jesus was born, captured the heart of Jewish ethics when he wrote: "Do not do to others what you do not want them to do to you." Jesus slightly reformulated Hillel's rule: "Do unto others as you would have them do unto you." We call it the Golden Rule. By stating this rule positively—do rather than don't do—Jesus widened its scope and impact. "Don't just refrain from doing evil," he was saying; "do good." Don't just refrain from hurting someone by stealing or killing or lying, but positively love and help them the way you would want to be loved and helped. Jesus said that the Law and the Prophets hinge upon this. The Apostle Paul, strictly schooled in Judaism as a Pharisee, summed it up to the early Christians in Rome like this: "Love doesn't do anything wrong to a neighbor; therefore, love is what fulfills the Law" (Romans 13:10). Christianity is steeped in Judaism, often without our realizing it. So much of what many Christians regard as Christian teaching is actually the Judaism that Jesus, Paul, and the other apostles grew up in and taught.

89

Atoning Sacrifice

The covenant that God made with Israel through Moses required, as part of the Law, offering animal sacrifices for atonement for sin. That observance continued all the way through Jesus' time.

After the construction of Solomon's Temple, it became the location for the Israelites' animal sacrifices. But the offering of animals ceased when the Romans destroyed the Second Temple in AD 70. That leads many Christians to wonder: If the sacrificial system was tied to atonement, and there are no more animal sacrifices, how do Jews find forgiveness today? How do they express thanksgiving?

My friend Rabbi Art Nemitoff of Temple B'nai Jehudah in Overland Park, Kansas, noted that, in the aftermath of the destruction of the temple, it was the "sacrifice of the heart" through liturgy and prayer that would henceforth be the means of atonement. This was consistent with the words of David in Psalm 51, "A broken spirit is my sacrifice, God. / You won't despise a heart, God, that is broken and crushed" (Psalm 51:17). God, speaking through the prophet Hosea said, "I desire faithful love and not sacrifice, / the knowledge of God instead of entirely burned offerings" (Hosea 6:6).

Judaism and the Afterlife

Because the afterlife is so important to Christian teaching—Paul told the Corinthians that, if there is no resurrection, their faith was in vain—Christians naturally are interested in what Jews believe on this subject. I posed this question to Rabbi Nemitoff, and he told me, essentially, that the answer depends on whom you ask. "You'll get a minimum of five answers," he said, "because there's no clear understanding [among Jews] of what the afterlife looks like."

We can see that divergence of opinion within the Judaism of Jesus' time. One group, the Sadducees, rejected the idea of resurrection. The Pharisees and others believed the dead would be raised and judged by God at the end of time. After the death of her brother, Lazarus, Martha references this belief when she says to Jesus, "I know that he will rise in the resurrection on the last day" (John 11:24). Today, Orthodox Jews believe in the resurrection. Many conservative Jews believe in an afterlife. Among Reform Jews, it is common to hear that we live on through our children, or through our legacy, or by being remembered by others after our death, though even among Reform Jews there are some who believe in a literal afterlife.

While there may be no definitive belief within Judaism today about the afterlife, Jews of all branches of Judaism agree that their faith is primarily focused on how one is to live here and now, not on what happens after we die.

Jews speak of heaven or the afterlife as *Olam Ha-Ba*: "the world to come." Rabbi Nemitoff noted, "We don't know what that looks like, but we believe that when we die our souls return to God and become part of Olam Ha-Ba. It is a heavenly garden of Eden." I find that to be a beautiful vision, and it's precisely the picture the Christian New Testament ends with. The Book of Revelation ends where the Book of Genesis began: in the garden of Eden where Paradise has been restored.

Rightly understood, Christianity is also focused primarily on this life. Christians have a clearer picture of the afterlife as both Jesus and the apostles spoke of the afterlife more freely than contemporary Judaism. But if you read the Gospels carefully, you'll discover that Jesus speaks of heaven far less than you might think. Like the Judaism he was a part of, his teaching is largely focused on how we should live as God's subjects. He calls his disciples not only to pray but also to act in such a way

91

that God's reign is experienced, and God's will is done, on earth as it is in heaven.

Where Judaism and Christianity Disagree

We'll end this chapter with a final word about where Jews and Christians find common ground, but before that let's briefly consider where Jews and Christians disagree.

The Nature of God

I asked Rabbi Nemitoff what God is like. He replied, "That is the $64,000 question. None of us know. We know that God is present in our life, just as we know that air exists because we are able to breathe. But I have never seen God. No one has ever seen God. So all we can do is believe." Rabbi Nemitoff and I would both agree that we can know something of God as we look at the world around us, and we can know something about God by the ways the biblical authors described God. And his words, "No one has ever seen God" reminded me of John 1:18, which also notes, "No one has ever seen God." But John goes on to say, "God the only Son, who is at the Father's side, has made God known." Christians believe that God came to humanity in Jesus to reveal himself to us. We see Jesus as the clearest picture of who God is and what God is like. When we read the Gospels and see Jesus forgiving sinners, healing the sick, delivering the oppressed, we believe we are seeing the character and heart of God. When we listen to Jesus' words in the Sermon on the Mount, his parables, and the rest of his teaching, we believe we are hearing the words and will of God. When we look at the cross of Christ, his suffering and death for the world, we believe we are seeing the redemptive, selfless love of God. When we think about Easter, Christ's resurrection, we see God's triumph over evil, sin, and death.

My Jewish friends acknowledge Jesus as a rabbi and a reformer, but not as the embodiment or incarnation of God.

This points to a second place of disagreement: Jews reject the Christian concept of the Trinity. When Jews hear Christians speak of God as Father, Son, and Spirit, it sounds like Christians are proclaiming that there are three gods, not one. As we'll see in the next chapter, this is a concern for Islam as well. I understand and appreciate the challenge the Trinity presents for Jews. Christians struggle to explain the idea. How God can be one, yet three distinct "persons," is a mystery. Christians believe that in Jesus God has come to us, and that through the Spirit, God works within us.

Christians see hints of the mystery of the Trinity in the Hebrew Bible. For instance, God uses the plural when speaking, "Let us make humanity in our image" (Genesis 1:26). There's also the fact that certain names for God, like Elohim, are plural, though usually used with singular verbs and adjectives. And there's the presence of the Spirit of God or the Spirit of the Lord who seems to be distinct from, yet one with, God. But Jews read each of these texts in ways that discount any possible trinitarian interpretations.

Christians reject the idea that the Trinity is a belief in three gods, but instead regard the Trinity as a way of understanding the nature of the one God both Jews and Christians believe in. But it is easy to understand why Jews struggle with this concept, given that most Christians struggle to make sense of it. It remains to Christians a mystery.

Jesus as Messiah

At the time Jesus arrived on the scene, the Messiah many Jews expected would be an earthly ruler who would return Israel to its former glory, or perhaps more, and usher in everlasting

93

peace. He would be not only a descendant of King David (as Jesus was) but would restore the throne of David. Jewish religious leaders could cite Scriptures, such as Isaiah 11, that pointed them in this direction.

But the earliest Christians, who were all Jews, saw that God had sent a different kind of Messiah, one who would reveal God's heart and character, who would beckon all people to know God, from the least to the greatest, who would transform hearts and lead us to pursue peace and to experience God's grace. This Messiah would reign in our hearts and transform the world one person at a time.

And Jesus' Jewish followers could go back into the Hebrew Bible and find Scriptures that they came to understand as prophetic clues about the kind of Messiah Jesus was truly to be. In the Psalms, Isaiah, Jeremiah, Zechariah, and other Scriptures, they saw prophetic foreshadowing of Jesus again and again. Jesus did not come as the kind of Messiah Jews were expecting. But he did come, Christians believe, as the kind of Messiah the world needed. My Jewish friends continue to pray and hope for the coming of the Messiah. Christians believe he has already come in Jesus.

A Great Deal in Common

Despite our differences, when I break bread with my Jewish friends, I find there is a deep kinship between us. My rabbi friends have a deep love for God, a deep desire to serve God, and a depth of understanding about the Scriptures that leaves me feeling grateful for their witness, insight, and friendship. As we talk about our ministry to our respective congregations I find, once more, that we share a great deal in common. We're each striving to help our congregants grow in their faith, to be motivated to serve God more fully in their daily lives, to love God with all their heart, soul, and might, and to love their neighbors as they love themselves.

We pray the same psalms. We read, in large part, the same Scriptures (more than two-thirds of the Christian Scriptures is the Hebrew Bible or "Old Testament"). We agree that there is one God, and he is God alone. We share together the call to "do justice, embrace faithful love, and walk humbly with [our] God" (Micah 6:8). And we share a commitment to living lives focused on helping our world look more like the kingdom of God. Which leads me to return to one last concept, important to multiple branches of Judaism, the concept of *tikkun olam*: healing or repairing the world.

Healing the World

Tikkun olam is not actually mentioned by name in the Hebrew Bible. But the idea behind the phrase as used by many in Reform and Conservative Judaism is a concept found throughout the Hebrew Bible.

It recognizes that there is a brokenness in the world that began when Adam and Eve chose to eat the forbidden fruit and this brokenness continues, as a result of our actions, to the present. It is seen everywhere the world does not look as God intended it to be, where there is suffering, injustice, or pain. Tikkun olam is the work of healing this brokenness. Doing justice, demonstrating mercy and compassion, serving others, practicing loving-kindness, these are all ways in which those Jews who emphasize tikkun olam see the mission of Judaism. It is the essence of God's call to Abraham to bless all the nations of the earth.

This same idea is behind most of Jesus' words in the Gospels. The parable of the good Samaritan and the parable of the sheep

95

and the goats are both about repairing the world. We are to feed the hungry, clothe the naked, give drink to the thirsty, visit the sick and imprisoned, and welcome the stranger. This is what love looks like according to Jesus.

Each week, Rabbi Nemitoff and I both give the benediction at the conclusion of worship in our respective congregations, sending our people out to live their faith in part by seeking to heal or repair the brokenness in our world. I want to challenge you to practice tikkun olam, to ask each day, "What can I do today to bring healing, hope, help, encouragement, kindness, or justice to my world?"

Earlier in this chapter I mentioned that there was a country club in Kansas City that did not allow Jewish people to join until the early 1990s. But I didn't tell you how it finally came to be changed.

The change happened because Tom Watson, one of the greatest golfers of all time, resigned his membership from the club in protest of the club's exclusionary policy. He said he would not play again at this club until it changed its policies. A few months later, the club admitted its first Jewish family into membership.

Sometimes, all it takes to help heal the world is one person to stand up for what is right and against what is wrong. If you are a disciple of Christ, my hope is that you would stand with your Jewish neighbors, coworkers, friends, and others when they face anti-Semitism of any kind. Doing this is one more way of healing the world.

Timeline
Islam and Christianity

Dates	Islam	Christianity
0		Life of Jesus (4 BC-AD 29)
		New Testament Written (AD 49-100 +/-)
		Earliest version of Apostles Creed in use (AD 200)
		Nicene Creed (AD 325)
AD 400		St. Augustine (AD 354-430)
AD 550	Muhammad is born (AD 570) Muhammad marries at age 25 (AD 595)	Council of Chalcedon (AD 451)
AD 600	Muhammad visited by Gabriel and begins reciting the Quran (AD 610)	Pope Gregory the Great (AD 590-604)
	Muhammad teaches the messages he receives (AD 610-632)	
	Muhammad and his followers move to Medina (ca. AD 622)	
	Muhammad leads an army and captures Mecca (AD 629)	
	Muhammad dies (AD 632)	
AD 650	Islam spreads rapidly throughout North Africa, the Middle East, and into Europe (AD 632-750)	Third Council of Constantinople (AD 680-681)
AD 700		
AD 750		
		Crusades (AD 1095-1291)

5.

ISLAM

To God Abraham said, "If only you would accept Ishmael!"

But God said, "No, your wife Sarah will give birth to a son for you, and you will name him Isaac. I will set up my covenant with him and with his descendants after him as an enduring covenant. As for Ishmael, I've heard your request. I will bless him and make him fertile and give him many, many descendants. He will be the ancestor of twelve tribal leaders, and I will make a great nation of him."

(Genesis 17:18-20)

I wrote the first edition of this book a year after 9/11, when the trauma of seeing the World Trade Center towers fall was still fresh on the mind of every American. Americans were afraid of an enemy we did not understand. What we did understand was that those who committed these heinous acts did so in the name of their religion. Each of the nineteen terrorists who participated in these attacks claimed to be a Muslim. Most of us knew little about Islam, but suddenly the entire religion was suspect, as were the world's 1.3 billion Muslims.

Did the 9/11 attackers represent all of Islam? Were they typical of the world's Muslim population?

In the days and weeks after the attack, a fear of Muslims swept over many in our country. Hate crimes against Muslims spiked. Americans had a difficult time differentiating between Muslims, Sikhs, and Hindus, leading to an increase in slurs and acts of hate toward people of a variety of faiths. At the same time, there were millions of Americans who addressed their fears by seeking to understand Islam and to get to know their Muslim neighbors who, they discovered, were living in fear as well.

My goal in writing the first edition of the book was to help Christians understand their neighbors of other faiths, in the hope that understanding would lead us away from fear and help us love our neighbors. As it related to Islam, I hoped to help readers understand the difference between Islamic extremism and Islam as practiced by the vast majority of the world's Muslims. I wanted to help readers find common ground with their Muslim neighbors, discover opportunities to learn from them, and ultimately befriend them.

Seventeen years later, fear of Muslims has risen to its highest level since September 11, 2001. Hate crimes against Muslims rose 15 percent in 2017 compared to 2016.[1] In Kansas City, just a couple of weeks before I wrote this chapter, an Islamic family arrived home to see smoke billowing from their garage. Someone had broken into the home while the mother, father, and their three children were out, lit a fire in the stairway, and spray-painted the words, "Allah Scum" inside the house.

Just a few months before this, three men were found guilty of seeking to set off bombs at a Garden City, Kansas, apartment complex where Muslim Somali immigrants were living as they worked in the area's meat packing industry. The three men, calling themselves "the Crusaders," intended to kill as many of the Somali workers as possible, along with their spouses and their children. These are two of hundreds of anti-Islamic incidents that happen each year. Seventeen years after 9/11, we're still in need of learning about our Muslim neighbors.

My first encounter with Muslims occurred when I was in high school. My father had taken a job working in Saudi Arabia, where he would spend seven years working for the national airline. During my junior year, he flew me over to spend a week with him. I'd never left the US before, and this was a remarkable experience for a kid from Kansas. We had coffee and dates at the Meridien Hotel overlooking the Persian Gulf. We ate shawarma from street vendors in downtown Dharhan. I met my dad's Saudi coworkers and friends.

Until then, I didn't know a single Muslim. Suddenly, I was immersed in a culture that was completely unfamiliar to me, but I found the people I met kind, warm, and welcoming.

In the years since then I've had the opportunity to spend time with Muslims in Turkey, Jordan, Egypt, and the West Bank. I've spent time with Islamic leaders in Kansas City, visited their religious services at area mosques, and read major portions of the Quran. I've broken bread with Muslims and listened to their stories. And I've read a great deal about Islam, both from its adherence and its detractors.

In this chapter we'll consider Islam's story, its fundamental beliefs, and the places Islam and Christianity disagree. We'll conclude with some common ground between the two faiths.

The Beginning of Islam:
Muhammad

Islam is the youngest of the world's five major religions. As with Buddhism, Islam begins with the story of one man. Muhammad lived about six hundred years after the time of Christ, from AD 570 to 632.

Muhammad was born in Mecca, on the western coast of what is now Saudi Arabia. Mecca was becoming an important center for trade and finance at the time, but it was best known for an ancient shrine to which the people of the Arabian Peninsula made pilgrimage. The shrine, still standing, is Islam's holiest site. It is called the Ka'bah (related to our word *cube*). It is roughly forty feet high by forty feet wide by thirty-four feet deep. Inside the Ka'bah (also spelled Kaaba), there were idols to each of the more than three hundred gods worshiped among the Arabian tribes. The shrine served to unite the disparate groups that called the Arabian Peninsula home.

While the shrine was intended for worship, Mecca was far from being a "holy city" when Muhammad was born there. It was notorious for its immorality.

Muhammad's early life was marked by tragedy. His father died a few months before his birth. His mother died when he was six or seven years old. He went to live with his grandfather, who passed away shortly thereafter. He spent the rest of his childhood years being raised by his uncle in Mecca. The family was respectable, and respected, but they were poor. With no opportunity for an education, Muhammad never learned to read or write.

But he learned about business. Because his uncle was a trader, Muhammad worked with the traders who came to Mecca. He accompanied his uncle in the great trade caravans

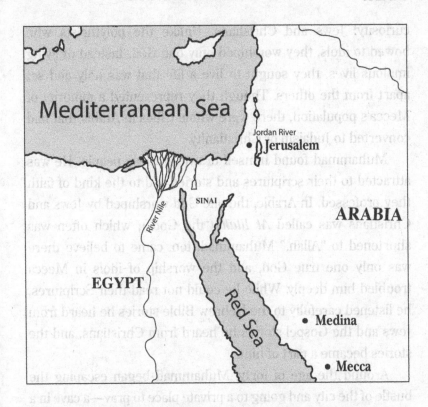

that crossed the Arabian Desert to and from Syria. He eventually became a merchant, known for his honesty and trustworthiness. His reputation was the opposite of the city where he lived. People knew they could take him at his word.

At the age of twenty-five, Muhammad married Khadijah, a wealthy widow, fifteen years his senior. The couple had six children: two boys who died in infancy, and four girls who survived. Muhammad remained married to Khadijah until her death twenty-four years later.

Even as he continued to develop as a businessperson, Muhammad began his search for God, especially after the deaths of his sons. He was both deeply spiritual and spiritually curious. Two groups in Mecca particularly piqued Muhammad's

103

curiosity: Jews and Christians. Unlike the polytheists who bowed to idols, they worshiped only one God. Instead of living impious lives, they sought to live a life that was holy and set apart from the others. Though they represented a minority of Mecca's population, there were whole tribes in Arabia that had converted to Judaism or Christianity.

Muhammad found himself drawn to these people. He was attracted to their scriptures and stories and to the kind of faith they professed. In Arabic, the one God worshiped by Jews and Christians was called *Al Illah* ("the God"), which often was shortened to "Allah." Muhammad, too, came to believe there was only one true God, and the worship of idols in Mecca troubled him deeply. While he could not read their Scriptures, he listened carefully to the Hebrew Bible stories he heard from Jews and the Gospel stories he heard from Christians, and the stories became a part of him.

Around the age of forty, Muhammad began escaping the bustle of the city and going to a private place to pray—a cave in a mountainside that overlooked Mecca. One day, as he was praying in this cave on Mount Hira, he had a profound experience. He felt a presence, and as though something were pressing against his chest. He heard a voice that said, "Recite!"

"Recite what?" Muhammad asked.

He heard the voice again: "Take and recite!"

"But what?" Muhammad asked again. The pressure on his chest became so great, he feared his chest would explode. Suddenly, he felt words coming to his heart. Then the words began springing from his lips—words he hadn't heard before. Terrified, he went back down into the city to find his wife. "I've either seen a demon, or I've seen an angel, or I'm losing my mind," he told her. "I don't know which."

After this experience he recited the words to friends, who wrote them down. These were the first of the sayings that eventually became the Quran (an Arabic word that means "recitations"). Over the next twenty-two years, until his death in 632, Muhammad continued to have these experiences, in which he believed the Angel Gabriel (called *Jibril* in Arabic) gave him messages from God.

Muhammad also continued to share the recitations with others, who wrote them down. And he began to preach and teach the messages he had received. Some thought he was going mad. Others considered him a false prophet. But some believed his teaching and accepted him as a prophet of God. At first, only his wife and a few members of his extended family followed Muhammad's words. Eventually, about forty families came to believe.

But in a city dominated by polytheists, the message that there is no god but "the God" and that the worship of idols was wrong was bound to generate hostility. Muhammad and his followers faced persecution in Mecca. In 622, there was a plot to assassinate him.

By this time, some of Muhammad's followers had moved to Medina, a city two hundred miles north of Mecca. As the situation in Mecca grew more dangerous for Muhammad, these believers invited him to move to their city, promising him their support. So he and his followers migrated to Medina, an event remembered by Muslims as the *Hegira* or the *Hijrah* (which means "migration").

Medina embraced Islam, marking the formation of the first Islamic community, and made Muhammad its leader. The city submitted to Islamic law and worshiped only the one God. Just as Christians measure history from the birth of Jesus (AD stands for *anno domini*, "the year of our Lord"), Muslims divide history according to the *Hijrah*. Thus, by Islamic reckoning, the year 2018 is 1439 AH, after the *Hijrah*.*

At this time, the revelations Muhammad claimed to receive from Gabriel began to focus on how to organize and run a city-state. The recitations also included words about how to address the conflicts with those who did not embrace their faith. These were both timely revelations. Muhammad was no longer just a religious teacher; he was becoming a political ruler, too, and so he received instructions on civic laws, keeping order, how inheritances should be governed, and what was right and wrong in God's sight.

At the same time, Muhammad and his followers found themselves constantly battling their opponents. Mecca and Medina were at war with each other. Various tribes were involved in the fighting. Sometimes various groups of Arabian Jews fought alongside Muhammad, and sometimes they fought against him. In the midst of this, Muhammad began to receive recitations about rules for warfare and how to treat enemies in battle. When we find violent passages in the Quran, they typically originated in this time when Muhammad and his men were regularly at war.

Muhammad proved to be a great warrior and military leader. He seems like Joshua in the Old Testament—in battle most of his life, and prevailing with God's help. At the end of AD 629, seven years after he had been driven out of his hometown, Muhammad led an army of ten thousand men against Mecca. They captured the city with little resistance. Muhammad cleansed the Ka'bah of its idols, destroyed the pagan statues, and declared an end to polytheistic worship. Claiming that the Ka'bah was originally built by Abraham (on top of the foundations of a shrine built

---

* Muslims use the lunar calendar rather than the solar calendar, so the years don't align with the way they're counted in the Gregorian calendar used in the West.

to honor God by Adam), he made it the single most important place of worship for Muslims, which it remains to this day.

Three years later, Muhammad died in Medina, where he is buried. From that time forward, Muslims took their faith throughout the world. Within one hundred years of Muhammad's death, Islam had spread like wildfire across North Africa, the entire Middle East, and into southern Europe.

Essential Muslim Beliefs

Islam's Creed: The Shahada

At the heart of Islam is a central affirmation or creed, called the *Shahada*. It is but one sentence in length, but it captures the essence of Islamic faith: "There is no God but Allah and Muhammad is his messenger [or prophet]." *Allah*, as we have learned, is the Arabic word for God used by Arabic Christians and Jews, as well as Muslims (just as *Dios* is the Spanish word for God). This affirmation is similar to the Shema in Judaism in its affirmation of the belief in one God, but obviously differs in the naming of Muhammad as God's messenger.

The word *Islam* is typically translated as "surrender" or "submission" and a Muslim (the word shares the same root as *Islam*) is one who submits or surrenders to God. Muslims pray on their knees, bowing all the way until their foreheads touch the ground. This is a sign of complete surrender of one's self to God, the only God, and complete submission to God's will.

In this idea of complete submission to God there is a deeply rooted connection with Judaism and with Christianity. In Arabic, the word *salaam*, from which the word *Islam* derives, can mean both "submission" and "peace." It suggests the inner peace we find when we surrender ourselves to God. It comes from the same Semitic root as the Hebrew word for peace: *shalom*.

107

This idea of submission to God is central to Christians. It is captured in the prayer John Wesley, Methodism's founder, invited his leaders to pray, known as the Wesley Covenant Prayer. Here is the essence of that prayer,

> I am no longer my own, but thine.
> Put me to what thou wilt, rank me with whom thou wilt.
> Put me to doing, put me to suffering.
> Let me be employed by thee or laid aside for thee,
> exalted for thee or brought low for thee.
> Let me be full, let me be empty.
> Let me have all things, let me have nothing.
> I freely and heartily yield all things
> to thy pleasure and disposal.[2]

Jews, Christians, and Muslims share in common this foundational belief in one God and in the conviction that to be authentically human is to submit one's life to God, and that in so doing, we find peace.

The Quran as God's Perfect Word

A second central affirmation of Muslims is that the Quran is God's word, and the only perfect record of God's will. While much of the Quran draws upon material in the Old and New Testaments, and the Quran mentions the Torah, the Psalms, and the gospel of Jesus multiple times as coming from God, Muslims believe these documents, as we have them, were distorted, added to or changed by Jews in the case of the Torah and Psalms, and by early Christians in the case of the gospel of Jesus. The Arabic term for this distortion is *tahrif*.

Muslims see the Quran as the definitive word of God, correcting errors in the Torah, Psalms, and gospel and offering God's word to the world. The Quran, for Muslims, literally contains the words of God, dictated by the angel Gabriel to

Muhammad over a twenty-three-year period of time. Since Muhammad could not write, he memorized these words, and then recited them to others who wrote them down. The word *Quran*, as we've already learned, means "recitation," and Muslims regard only the Quran in Arabic as the words of God. In other words, the true recitations of God's words can only be in Arabic, as this is the language in which the angel gave these words to Muhammad. Any translation is just that, someone's translation of the words of God.

The various recitations Muhammad received and passed on were collected after Muhammad's death and became the Quran. There are 114 chapters, called *surahs*. The surahs are further divided into verses. There are over 6,000 verses in the Quran.

During their daily times of prayer, Muslims recite the Quran. Memorizing the entire Quran is a requirement for becoming an *imam*, a teacher in a mosque. Because they believe the Quran contains the actual words of God, a Muslim would never set a Quran on the floor or even allow it to gather dust on a coffee table.

When opening the Quran, we might expect the surahs to be arranged by theme, or chronologically, but instead they are arranged by length, from the longest to the shortest. The entire collection is slightly shorter than the New Testament.

Christians will recognize much in the Quran. Its content demonstrates how much Muhammad was influenced by the Jews and Christians he knew and by their Scriptures. Gabriel, whom Muhammad claimed gave him the words of the Quran to recite, is the Gabriel who announced to Mary in the New Testament that she would give birth to Jesus. In fact, there is an entire surah about Mary. There are also stories about Abraham, Sarah, Isaac, Ishmael, Moses, Noah, Jonah, David, and Solomon. Jesus is mentioned more than seventy times in the Quran.

Yet if many of the characters in the Quran are familiar to Christians and Jews, their stories often do not align with those we find in the Hebrew Bible and the New Testament. For Muslims, whenever there is disagreement between the Quran and Jewish or Christian Scripture, the Quran is correct because it is the definitive word of God. As Muhammad understood it, some of the revelations from God that he received were given to rectify the mistakes of Jews and Christians, who also had received revelations but, as noted above, had garbled and corrupted them. The Quran was the error-free version of God's original word. But because Jews, Christians, and Muslims all looked to scriptures to understand God's word, Muhammad regarded all of them as "people of the book."

The Five Pillars of Islam

Within the Quran are five foundational practices, called the Five Pillars, that define what it means to be Muslim.

1. **Shahada:** *Confession of faith.* While the Quran is the foundation beneath Islam, the single most important part of being a Muslim is confessing one's faith. As we saw above, Islam focuses on one simple faith statement: "I bear witness to this truth. There is no God but Allah, and Muhammad is his prophet." If you confess this and believe it in your heart, Islam regards you as a Muslim.

2. **Salat:** *Prayer.* Five times a day, Muslims kneel in prayer. They face Mecca, bowing their heads all the way to touch the ground, and recite portions of the Quran as they pray.

3. **Zakat:** *Giving to the poor.* The word *Zakat* means "that which purifies" and it is a required offering—

something like a tax—given to help the poor and
needy, new converts, and others. The amount is
approximately 2.5 percent of one's wealth each year.
This is not simply 2.5 percent of one's income, but of
one's accumulated wealth.

4. **Sawm:** *Fasting during Ramadan.* Once a year,
Muslims fast from dawn to dusk for an entire month.
The Ramadan fast, which is lifted each evening at
sunset, commemorates the first vision that was given
to Muhammad. It also marks the *Hijrah*, the flight
from Mecca to Medina. Ramadan is the ninth month of
the Islamic calendar; the starting time depends on the
appearance of the new moon.

5. **Hajj:** *Pilgrimage to Mecca.* If they are physically
able and can afford it, Muslims are to make the
pilgrimage to Mecca once in a lifetime where they
will circumambulate (walk around) the Ka'bah seven
times. This journey is a profound experience of unity
with other Muslims. Muslims may make the journey
at any time, but there is one particular month (the
month of Hajj) when Muslims from all over the world
travel to Mecca.

It's not hard to see the points of connection between these
Five Pillars and Christianity. Christians believe in one God. We
believe in the importance of prayer (Paul taught us to "pray
without ceasing"). We believe that helping the poor is a mandate
from God. We believe in fasting, especially during the forty
days of Lent (some Christians also fast one day each week).
And though it is not a requirement, many Christians make
pilgrimages to the Holy Land to walk in the places that Jesus
walked. Perhaps, then, it should not be surprising that, in the

Quran, God says to Muslims, "You will find the nearest in love to the believers (Muslims) are those who say, 'We are Christians'" (al-Maa'idah 5:82).

Essential Differences
Between Christianity and Islam

Despite some of the similarities I have described, there are also areas where Christians and Muslims see things in profoundly different ways.

Islam on Jesus Christ

According to the Quran, Jesus (*Isa* in Arabic) was born to Mary, a virgin, just as we find in the New Testament. He worked miracles. He taught with wisdom and with understanding. He was the Jewish Messiah (al-Masih). On all of this Christians and Muslims agree.

Muslims view Jesus as a great prophet—the most important prophet, in fact, up until Muhammad, whom they understand as God's greatest and final prophet. After they say Jesus' name, Muslims reflexively add, "Peace be upon him," just as they do when they say Muhammad's name. In these ways, Islam comes closer than Judaism to Christianity in recognizing Jesus' identity and importance.

But this is as far as Islam can go. Muhammad rejected as false teaching some of the central assertions of the earliest Christians, who understood Jesus as much more than a prophet. Islam, like Judaism, claims that the apostles distorted the faith.

For Muhammad, Jesus was not the Word of God made flesh. He was in no sense divine. He was not Emmanuel—God with us. He was not the Savior of the world. He did not die on a cross to atone for or redeem the world from its sins, or to demonstrate the depth of God's love for us. In fact, he did not die on a cross at all;

according to Islam, someone else died in Jesus' place, as Jesus was instead taken up to heaven, avoiding the cross. Because Jesus did not undergo a physical death, he would not have said to his disciples at the Last Supper, "This is my body and my blood." And since Jesus did not die, there was no resurrection in which he triumphed over suffering, violence, and death.

For Muhammad, Christian doctrine may have seemed confusing. Some Christian scholars have suggested that Muhammad did not completely understand the claims of the Christian faith. For example, to someone fighting against polytheism, as Muhammad was, the idea of the Trinity may have sounded a lot like a belief in multiple gods. As noted in the last chapter, Christians themselves often have a hard time explaining the Trinity. And if there is no Trinity, then how could God have been born as a human child, delivered by a human mother? And how could God have died a human death on a cross? So Islam rejects all of these doctrines that are central to the Christian faith. Muslims believe these were distortions to the gospel of Jesus made by Paul and other early apostles.

This rejection of Jesus' death on the cross seems particularly odd to Christians, given that all of the earliest witnesses to Jesus focus on his death on a Roman cross. The Gospels were all first-century documents testifying to Christ's death. Yet six hundred years later, Muhammad claimed that these Christians were in error and that Jesus was not crucified.

The Bible and the Quran

For our Muslim cousins, the Quran is God's final, definitive word: God's revelation to human beings. Christians can accept that there are some beautiful things written in the Quran, and much that is consistent with the Old and New Testaments. But Christians and Jews do not believe that the Quran was dictated by the Angel Gabriel to Muhammad. And Christians do not

113

believe that God's ultimate revelation was a book; instead we believe that God's Word became flesh in Jesus. Muslims believe the Word of God became a book. Christians believe the Word of God came to us through the person of Jesus.

How do Christians explain Muhammad's experiences in receiving his revelations? We look at them in much the same way that we explain our own religious experiences. Many of us have moments when we feel God speaking to us.

As a pastor, after twenty-eight years of trying to hear God speak and attempting to speak on God's behalf week after week, here is what I have learned: Even the best of us are spiritually hard of hearing. I devote twenty hours a week to reading, praying, researching, and writing my sermons, but I have never heard God speak to me in an audible voice. Instead, I feel something in my heart, which I think is what Muhammad felt when he experienced the first recitation pressed upon his chest in that cave on the mountainside. As someone who is spiritually hard of hearing, I know that sometimes I can mishear. I can get things wrong. I find that when people believe that God is speaking to them, or pressing something onto their hearts, they filter it through their own understanding, their own cultural situation, presuppositions, questions, and concerns. And those filters can affect the word that preachers and other hard-of-hearing Christians deliver.

I came to faith in a little Pentecostal church. In Pentecostal churches, there is a heavy emphasis on the ability of the Holy Spirit to speak directly to the individual believer. People are expected to have moments when the Spirit prompts them to deliver a message. I distinctly remember the middle of one worship service, when a man stood up during the middle of a hymn. He believed the Spirit was speaking to him; the congregation stopped singing, and the room grew quiet. And then the man declared, "Thus sayeth the Lord, 'As in the days

of Moses, when he built the ark in preparation for the flood…'"
And he went on from there.

Even as a teen, I realized that what he was saying didn't line up with the stories in my Bible. I wondered, "Did God forget that it was Noah, not Moses, who built the ark?"

The experience taught me early on that we may feel God speaking to us, but that message is heard in the light of our presuppositions and our cultural setting and is still processed by our head and heart. Our own biases and assumptions, or even our own confusion or lack of knowledge, get in the way of accurately hearing from God. It happens to me. Sometimes I feel a strong conviction about something that I believe is God's word. But in those moments I know I need to ask myself, "Is this God, or is it me?"

In the New Testament we find the same call for a "reality check" among the apostles. As the writer of 1 John cautions: "Dear friends, don't believe every spirit. Test the spirits to see if they are from God" (1 John 4:1). We test them against the witness and example of Jesus.

I think Muhammad earnestly believed that what he recited for others came, word-for-word, from God. But Muhammad was also a man, and whatever he heard was necessarily through fallible human ears. It was filtered through his own theology, presuppositions, questions, doubts, and historical setting. Those included things he had gleaned from hearing Christian and Jewish Scriptures. They included the animosity he had seen and observed from, and between, Christians and Jews.

There are things in the Quran about which I and my Muslim neighbors can stack hands and say, "That's right!" But there are other places where, as a Christian, I have to say, "We don't see this matter the same way." I accept that we will disagree. Families regularly disagree, even on some fundamental issues. They still love each other. They can still sit down together over

Thanksgiving dinner. Figuring out how to have conversations with others in the human family over things about which we disagree is important to our ability to live in the world with other human beings. And it's critically important to any who wish to be "ambassadors for Christ."

Islam and Violence

Our disagreements lead me to the question many Christians ask about Muslims: is Islam a religion of violence? They hear terms like *jihad* and see news about people who call themselves *jihadis* committing acts we would call terrorism. They read certain passages about war from the Quran, often quoted by Islam's detractors, that would rightly leave us anxious if they capture the faith accurately. They have seen examples of violence in the name of Islam that leave them with a suspicion that is hard to shake, no matter how many times they have been reassured that Islam is a religion of peace (and, as you will recall, derives its very name from a word for peace). Indelibly etched in the minds of many Americans are the images of airplanes flying into buildings while people shout "God is great!" in Arabic. On top of that, there are opponents of Islam who create "jihad watch" websites and disseminate information to play on people's fears, thereby adding to a distorted picture of Islam.

Is Islam a religion of violence? Should you be afraid of Muslims in your community? Let's consider a few facts. In the years since 9/11, there have been an average of nine people killed each year in America at the hands of Islamic extremists.[3] This, in a nation of over 300 million people. Statistically, you are hundreds of times more likely to die choking on your own food this year than to die at the hands of an Islamic terrorist.[4] Each year there are violent attacks perpetrated by extremists. You are twice as likely to be killed by a non-Muslim right wing extremist

116

than by a Muslim.[5] My point is that we have associated a small violent group of extremists with over 3 million Muslims who live in our country.

I think about Westboro Baptist Church in Topeka, Kansas. This is a very small church that is known across the country for picketing the funerals of servicemen and servicewomen and of gay people with messages of hate. Do they reflect Christianity? Do the members of the Ku Klux Klan or other hate groups who cover their hate in Christian rhetoric and symbols represent the Christian faith? Were the Crusades, or the religious wars in Europe, or the pogroms against the Jews faithful expressions of the Christian faith—the faith whose leader calls us to love our enemies? In the same way, violent Islam does not reflect the faith of the vast majority of Muslims.

Consider another question related to violence in the Quran. What are we to do when a holy book calls for a father to put his wife or children to death if they worship another god? Or if it advocates burning children alive who become prostitutes? Or if it calls for the wholesale killing of men, women, and children in cities who do not worship the true God? Or if it commands the death penalty for disobedience to parents or engaging in premarital sex? These are all examples not from the Quran but from the Old Testament.

When we read those passages, we read them in the light of their historical context and we don't take them as license to act in similar ways today. This is precisely how most of the world's Muslims read similar passages in the Quran.

Jesus offers us God's definitive word as it relates to violence, a word I believe was far closer to the heart of God than what we find in the passages condoning, or at times commanding, violence in either the Torah or the Quran. His instructions about violence and how one responds to enemies need no special context for us to understand them. He taught us to *love* our enemies, to

117

pray for those who persecute us, and to turn the other cheek. He hung on a cross and prayed for his Father to forgive those who hung him there. Paul and the other apostles also taught this love of enemies and demonstrated mercy, as when Paul wrote to urge the Christians of Rome, "Don't be defeated by evil, but defeat evil with good" (Romans 12:21).

Christianity, Islam, and every other religion have both good interpreters of the faith and bad ones. There are extremists among them all, including Buddhists, Hindus, Jews, and Christians. Just as I fervently believe that hate groups and extremists who use the name of Christ to justify their hate do not accurately represent Christianity, the vast majority of Muslims believe violent extremists do not represent Islam.

Is Islam a religion of violence? No. There are extremists who claim to be Muslim who use violence to accomplish their goals. This is tragic. But they do not reflect the Muslims I've encountered in the Middle East, or those in my own community, who have demonstrated nothing but humility, hospitality, and kindness to me.

Christ's Ambassadors

I am unabashedly, unequivocally a Christian. I believe that Jesus was more than a prophet. I believe that he suffered and died on a cross and was resurrected to life. I believe that he is the clearest picture of the truth about God. *And* I care about Muslims, and have been inspired to be a better Christian by spending time with Muslims I know. I'll give you a few examples.

The Muslim path of praying five times a day inspired me to pray more. The Muslim practice of reciting the Quran during prayers led me to use the Christian Scriptures as the basis of my prayers more regularly. The Islamic pillar of giving to the poor led LaVon and me to increase the percentage of our income we give to the poor. Devout Muslims helped make me a more devoted Christian.

After I preached a sermon on Islam and Christianity earlier this year, a Muslim woman—a leader of the Islamic community—approached me in the narthex of our church. She said she lives not far from the church, and she drives past it regularly with her children. She said she wondered as she would drive by: "Are the people in this church the kind of Christians we have to be afraid of?" She went on to say that it was her first time to visit, and she had felt the warmth and welcome of our congregation. "It felt so good to hear you talk about my faith in a way that was charitable and fair" she said, "and for you to try to understand me and to express care for Muslims. Thank you!"

Paul writes, "We are ambassadors for Christ, since God is making his appeal through us" (2 Corinthians 5:20 NRSV). What kind of ambassador for Christ will you be to your Muslim neighbors? Will you be fearful of them, ignore them, or insult their faith? Or will you befriend them, get to know them, and treat them with respect, compassion, and kindness? If your response is the latter, you have begun to understand and to live the gospel of Jesus Christ.

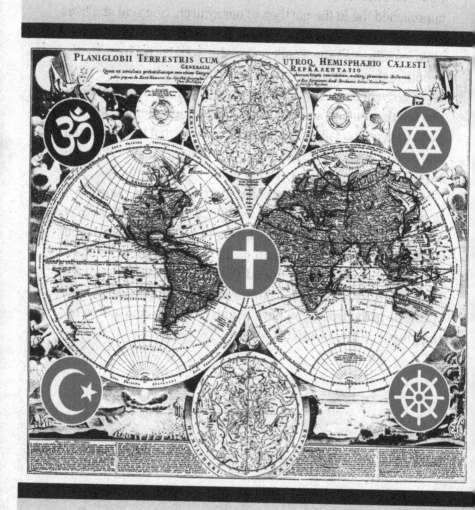

6.

CHRISTIANITY

God so loved the world that he gave his only Son, so that everyone who believes in him won't perish but will have eternal life.

(John 3:16)

On Super Bowl Sunday in 2018, Toyota ran a commercial called "One Team." It begins with a rabbi leaving his synagogue and hopping into his (Toyota) pickup truck. He then stops by to pick up a priest just after mass. Together they stop to pick up a Muslim imam at his mosque, toying with him a bit as he seeks to get in the car. Finally, they pick up a Buddhist monk. With shared esprit de corps they make their way to a football game, met in the stands by two nuns who chide them for being late. They cheer together as their team scores a touchdown. And then the message of the ad flashes across the screen: "We're all one team." (Do a Google search for it. It's worth watching!)

I loved this spot. It captures the ideal of people of different faiths being able to have fun and fellowship together and to be friends and neighbors who share something in common despite their differences. And that is part of the point of this book.

But the message of the ad also raises an interesting question: *Are* we all on one team?

It depends on how you look at it. On the one hand, the two teams that competed in that Super Bowl—the Philadelphia Eagles and New England Patriots—weren't all one team. They battled hard against each other. They each wanted badly to win, which meant that someone had to lose.

On the other hand, after the game was over, the players on the opposing teams all shook hands. They congratulated each other on a well-played game. Tom Brady, quarterback of the losing team, hugged the necks of Eagles players. They all had a lot of important things in common. They're all NFL players. They're all trying to be the best they can at what they do. They're all Americans. They're all human beings. From that perspective, they are all one team.

When it comes to world religions, it is clear that in many ways people of different faiths are on different teams. And yet, we share some important things in common as well. We're all human beings trying to find answers to the deepest questions of our existence. There is a place to be clear, compassionate, and humble about our differences. And there is a place for us to focus on what we share in common and to befriend and care for one another just as the clergy in the Toyota commercial or the NFL players from opposing teams after the big game.

Christian Beginnings

In chapter 4, we studied Judaism and came to see its major tenets, texts, and expressions. Christianity didn't begin as a separate religion but as a part of first-century Judaism. In some

122

ways, it could be seen as a renewal movement within Judaism, and the earliest Christians saw it as the fulfillment of the prophecies, hopes, and promises of the Jewish people.

In 2 Samuel 7:16, the prophet Nathan tells King David that God declared that David's throne—his dynasty—would continue forever. Thus began a hope that was nurtured and sustained among the Jewish people—even when their people were oppressed, in exile, or ruled over by foreign powers—that the day would come when God would raise up a descendant of David to rule over his people and to restore the nation to its rightful place as God's kingdom on earth, serving as a light to the nations.

In Hebrew, the king was often called *Messiah*, meaning "anointed one"—someone who would be anointed with oil and set apart as God's king. Many of the prophets seized upon this idea and assured the people that, despite exile, oppression, and foreign rule, God would one day send a messianic figure to deliver them and lead them.

Around the time of the birth of Jesus, there were many who were waiting, praying, and hoping for the Messiah to come, dispel the Romans as well as their client kings, usher in an era of peace, and lead a religious revival among the people. Others, who benefitted from the status quo through arrangements with the Romans, were not as excited about the old prophecies.

Around 4 BC, a peasant girl from the little village of Nazareth, engaged to a humble woodworker and handyman named Yosef, gave birth to a child in the small town of Bethlehem, just south of Jerusalem—the same town King David had been born in 1,000 years earlier. Both the child's mother and father were descendants of David. They named the child *Yeshua* in Aramaic, a name that means "salvation." We know him as Jesus.

Christians believe that this child was the long-awaited Messiah. He was not only born from Mary, who was a descendant of David; he was born in David's home town. He began his public ministry at the age of 30 (Luke 3:23), just as David became king at the age of 30 (2 Samuel 5:4). The primary focus of Jesus' preaching and teaching was the kingdom of God.

Yet he was not at all like the Messiah most Jews were expecting and hoping for. Jesus didn't seek to raise up an army to cast out the Romans. Instead, he called his followers to love their enemies, pray for those who persecuted them, and turn the other cheek when they were struck. He refused to take up arms against anyone. He showed little concern for restoring an earthly kingdom or garnering for himself any earthly power.

Jesus ministered and preached for about three years. Most of his ministry took place in and around the Sea of Galilee with occasional journeys beyond. Matthew, one of the four Gospel writers, summed up Jesus' ministry with these words:

Jesus traveled among all the cities and villages, teaching in their synagogues, announcing the good news of the kingdom, and healing every disease and every sickness. Now when Jesus saw the crowds, he had compassion for them because they were troubled and helpless, like sheep without a shepherd.

(Matthew 9:35-36)

The Gospels (Matthew, Mark, Luke, and John) are first-century descriptions of the life, ministry, teachings, death, and resurrection of Jesus. They describe Jesus as a healer who regularly stopped whatever else he was doing to heal the sick. He was a teacher who often taught in parables—short stories intended to teach about God and what it meant to live under God's rule as citizens of God's kingdom. His ethics are most clearly laid out in the Sermon on the Mount, found in Matthew chapters 5 through 7.

124

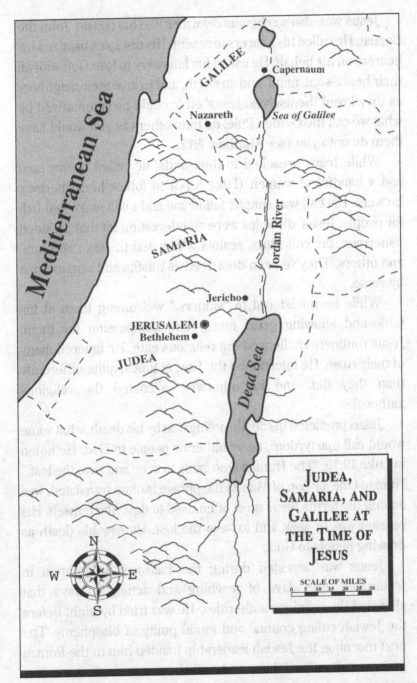

JUDEA, SAMARIA, AND GALILEE AT THE TIME OF JESUS

SCALE OF MILES
0 5 10 15 20 25 30

Jesus was also a religious reformer like his cousin, John the Baptist. He called his hearers to repent. His disciples baptized his hearers on his behalf. He called his followers to love God with all their heart, soul, mind, and strength, and to love their neighbors as they loved themselves. Jesus' ethic could be summarized by what we call the Golden Rule: do unto others as you would have them do unto you (see Matthew 7:12).

While Jesus preached to thousands, he called twelve men and a handful of women (Luke 8:1-3) to follow him wherever he went. His call was simple: follow me and I will make you fish for people. Jesus' disciples were an interesting lot that included fishermen, tax collectors, zealots who hated the tax collectors, and others. They've been described as misfits and ragamuffins by some.

While he ministered to "sinners," welcoming them at his table and showing great mercy and compassion for them, Jesus routinely challenged the religious elite. He ignored many of their rules. He interpreted the Law, at times, quite differently than they did, and he otherwise alienated the religious authorities.

Jesus predicted his death, noting that by his death, what some would call martyrdom, he would draw people to God. He noted in Luke 19:10, "The Human One came to seek and save the lost." Human One, or Son of Man as the phrase is often translated, was among the terms Jesus most often used to describe himself. His passion was to seek and to save the lost. He saw his death as drawing people to God.

Jesus was arrested during the Passover celebration in Jerusalem, after days of teaching and acting in ways that alienated the religious authorities. He was tried by night before the Jewish ruling council and found guilty of blasphemy. The next morning, the Jewish leadership handed him to the Roman governor, Pontius Pilate, and called for the death sentence, which Pilate ultimately pronounced. Jesus was sentenced to die at the hands of the Roman soldiers, death by crucifixion.

Jesus was crucified on Good Friday, and his body was hastily buried that afternoon and remained in the grave Friday and Saturday. But early in the morning on the following Sunday, what we call Easter today, the stone that had been placed in front of the tomb was rolled away. Jesus, now very much alive, stepped out of the tomb.

Some struggle with the healing miracles of Christ, but the idea of the Resurrection seems so utterly impossible that many reject it out of hand. The case for believing it rests with the testimony of the earliest eyewitnesses; the impact the Resurrection had on those early Christians; and Jesus' continuing appearances, following the Resurrection, including a dramatic appearance to Saul of Tarsus, better known as the Apostle Paul. There was, further, the empty tomb. But ultimately, at least to me, the case for belief in the Resurrection has more to do with the logic of the Resurrection. If Jesus were, in fact, from God, or in some sense divine as Christians believe, his death would have been a tremendous defeat of all that is good and of God himself. But the Resurrection would indicate that evil, hate, sin, and death do not have the final word. Instead, they are all defeated. This is why Easter signifies the ultimate triumph of hope.

The early Christians proclaimed that Jesus was in fact a very different kind of Messiah from what most people had expected. He wasn't the kind of Messiah many wanted, but he was the kind of Messiah everyone needed. Christians call Jesus: Messiah, King, Savior, and Lord (Lord, like King, signifies the highest authority, before whom all of his followers yield their hearts, obedience, and lives).

Forty days after his death and resurrection, before Jesus left his disciples one final time, he commissioned them to go into the world, continue his ministry, and teach and baptize others.

The early apostles did just this, taking Jesus' story and his teachings across the known world. In addition to preaching, some of the apostles composed letters to individuals and to churches, addressing the needs and questions of those churches and individual believers. These letters, called Epistles, represent twenty-two of the documents in the New Testament (if Revelation is counted as an Epistle—it is written as such to a handful of churches in modern-day Turkey). The earliest written Christian Scriptures, in addition to the Hebrew Bible, were the letters of Paul, the first of which was likely written around AD 49. The first of the Gospels was written in the sixties or seventies, and the last of them written around AD 90.

I'd like to devote the rest of this chapter to unpacking the good news of the Christian faith by turning to one of the best-known verses in all the New Testament. At the risk of seeming overly simplistic, but in part because it forms a great and memorable outline of Christian faith, I'd like to turn to John 3:16.

The Gospel in Miniature

It may seem trite or cliché to look at Christian faith through the lens of John 3:16, the Scripture often held up on signs in the end zone of football games, but the great reformer Martin Luther once called this verse, "the gospel in miniature." Perhaps you could read it aloud: "For God so loved the world, that he gave his only begotten Son, that whosoever believeth in him should not perish, but have everlasting life" (KJV).

In this brief passage we have an outline of Christian theology: a summary of the Christian view of the nature and character of God, of the human condition, and of the meaning and means of salvation. And we have Christianity's answer to four of the deepest existential questions human beings ask:

128

1. Am I loved?
2. Is there a purpose to life?
3. Can I be forgiven?
4. Is there hope?

Let's take a little time to unpack this passage of Scripture, phrase by phrase.

God So Loved the World

The passage begins with God, just as the Bible does in the first verse of Genesis: "In the beginning God created the heaven and the earth" (KJV). Christians believe in God. We believe that the universe did not come into existence by its own volition. Instead, the universe was called into being by the mind, will, and creative force of God. Creation testifies to the beauty, power, and grace of the Creator.

Many Christians believe that science offers us a compelling description of the forces at work in our universe and the processes by which life developed on our planet. We don't believe these disprove God's existence, but rather, they help us see how God created all that exists. It was a Catholic priest and physicist who proposed the big bang theory of the beginning of the universe. But before the big bang some 13.7 billion years ago, Christians believe there was God, who said, "Let there be light" (Genesis 1:3). God not only created but also sustains the universe. The physics upon which our universe exists, and the biological software that is behind life as we know it, were ultimately composed by God. And if the expanding universe collapses onto itself, as some astrophysicists believe it will billions of years from now, God will still be there.

Christians are not alone in this belief. While Buddhists are agnostic when it comes to God, Hinduism, Judaism, and Islam all share the belief that there is One who created the world around us. In fact, through recorded history, the vast majority of human beings have believed there is a being higher than themselves.

What Is God Like?

Various religions answer this question in different ways, sharing some beliefs and differing in others. For Christians, John 3:16 summarizes the answer in the first phrase: "God so loved the world."

Christians believe that one of the defining qualities of God's character, the quality that tells us more about God's nature than any other, is love. This points to a second attribute of God: personhood. In fact, God defines personhood. When the Bible indicates that humanity was created in the image of God, it is not telling us that we physically *look like* God. It is pointing to our spirit, our rational mind, our capacity to love and be in relationship with others. We believe that God is also holy, righteous, just, and kind, but underlying all of these attributes is love.

As we understand it, God's love is not simply a warm and caring feeling. It is a fundamental orientation, a way of being and acting. In the Old Testament we frequently find a Hebrew word, *chesed*, to describe this love. It often translates as steadfast love or covenant love. But it also translates as mercy—demonstrating kindness for its own sake, not because it is earned or deserved (and sometimes when it clearly is not deserved). The very fact of our existence as human beings is due to the *chesed* of God.

In the New Testament we find the Greek word *agape*. It has a meaning that is similar to *chesed* in the sense that it is not simply about emotions or feelings, but a love that takes action—extending kindness, seeking the good of the other, even at some

130

personal cost. And, like *chesed*, it means a type of love that cannot be earned; in this the word is sometimes translated as "mercy" or "charity" because it signifies undeserved kindness or blessings. But even beyond mercy, *agape* means selfless, sacrificial love. It is the kind of love that is willing to turn the other cheek, to love one's enemies, to love without any expectation of repayment. It is the kind of love that, in Paul's description, "believes all things, hopes all things, endures all things" (1 Corinthians 13:7 NRSV). *Agape* is the nature and character of God.

First John 4:8 says it plainly, "God is love." For Christians, God is certainly more than just love, but God is never *less* than love.

He Gave His Only Begotten Son

After that initial phrase, the "gospel in miniature" moves quickly to focus on the person of Jesus. The first phrase of John 3:16 tells us that God exists and that God loves us; the second phrase tells us how God demonstrated his love in a most extraordinary way. The Christian gospel is the story of God's love written large through the life, teachings, death, and resurrection of Jesus. To express this love God did not send a book, as in Islam's view of the Quran. Neither did God send another prophet or law-giver, though in a sense Jesus was both of these. No, Christians believe God came in human flesh. We call this the Incarnation—the enfleshment of God. John writes in his Gospel (1:14 NRSV): "The Word became flesh and lived among us."

Some Hindus consider Jesus an avatar or deity. Some forms of Buddhism look upon Jesus as a Boddhisatva—an enlightened being who helps others reach enlightenment. Many Jews consider Jesus a great rabbi and reformer. Muslims regard him as a prophet and the Jewish Messiah. They think of him as they think of Muhammad, and as Buddhists think of the Buddha, and as Jews think of Moses: human beings who did extraordinary things. Christians say that Jesus was much more.

The Incarnation was not merely the appearance of God in human form, as with manifestations of the deity in Hinduism or like the actors Morgan Freeman and George Burns, who each played God in Hollywood movies. Instead, in Jesus God actually took on our humanity. The church has always struggled to find just the right words to describe this mystery. The divine was united with human flesh in Jesus' conception, his birth, his life, and his death. The God who created the universe came to us, as one of us, in an effort to finally and definitively make himself known to humanity, to draw humankind to himself, and to redeem and deliver us from our brokenness, lostness, grief, pain, and sin. Jesus was God's response to the human condition—to our need for hope, love, forgiveness, meaning, light, and life.

As I was writing this chapter, I was caring for a family in my congregation who had just lost their twenty-one-year-old daughter in a tragic accident. My heart has been breaking for them. I spent time with the family. I officiated at the service. I've followed up and been in regular prayer for them. But as much compassion and care as I've felt for them, I know I cannot fully understand what they are going through. I can imagine it, but I don't really know. I've never lost a child. We have a grief group at the church for parents who lose children, because we know that the most helpful care someone receives at such a terrible loss is usually from someone who has walked in their shoes.

When I think of the Christian gospel, the assertion that God actually came to us and experienced our humanity, I am reminded of God's desire to actually walk in our skin. He chose to be born, to live in poverty, to experience the full range of things we experience—temptation, loneliness, heartache, joy, sorrow, love, betrayal, fear, pain, and death. God knows and understands because God the Son became flesh and walked on this earth, experiencing our humanity.

Because he was fully human, Christians sometimes refer to him as "Christ our brother." He experienced the full range of human feelings and emotions. But he came not only to know our life and experience, he came that we might know him—his heart, character, and will. Everything Jesus says and does in his ministry helps us see who God is, what God is like, and what God's will is for our lives.

Because Jesus was divine, he was able to open the eyes of the blind, make the lame to walk, cast out demons and mental illness, calm the waters in the midst of storms, and even raise the dead. He did the very things we would expect him to do if somehow God had come to us in him. The New Testament notes of him, "No one has ever seen God. It is God the only Son, who is close to the Father's heart, who has made him known" (John 1:18 NRSV). Likewise in Colossians 1:15 we read, "The Son is the image of the invisible God." Jesus said it this way, "Whoever has seen me has seen the Father" (John 14:9). So when we pray to God, whom we have not seen, we think of Jesus, who lived among us. He came as God's love letter in human flesh, a love letter written large for the world.

Notice the kinds of people on whom Jesus focused. He spent most of his time with those who were lost or broken, written off by the rest of the community as hopeless causes, or made to feel that they didn't matter. He spent time with sinners and prostitutes, the lepers and the unclean. He was constantly reaching out to them to say, "You matter to God. You are loved." (In the process, of course, he was also teaching everyone else that these people matter to God and should be treated accordingly.)

133

Jesus Loves Me, This I Know

In Dr. Martin Luther King Jr.'s sermon "A Knock at Midnight" he notes, "Everybody wishes to love and be loved. He who feels that he is not loved feels that he does not count." This is our deepest existential need as human beings: to know that we are loved. It is one of the existential questions that all religions seek to address. And Christianity testifies that Jesus came to show people—not just in general but as individuals—God's emphatic answer: you are loved. It doesn't matter who you are. It doesn't matter what you have done in the past. Jesus came as an expression of God's love to understand the depth of God's love for each of us.

The great twentieth-century theologian Karl Barth wrote a series of books on systematic theology. These volumes are so dense and detailed they occupy three feet of space on a bookshelf. Yet someone once asked the brilliant theologian if he could summarize the gospel. Here is what he said: "Jesus loves me this I know, for the Bible tells me so."

Barth rightly recognized that this is not simply the stuff of children's songs, nor is it a mere platitude. Its implications are enormous. When I preach the message that "God loves you," I know that some of the people in the congregation are walking through difficult times, feeling that they are not loved. They feel that their lives don't matter to anyone. That's one of the factors behind the epidemic of suicides in our country today. But even if you feel that no one else loves you, God says, "I love you." God says, "I have called you by name. You are one of my children." God says, "I know all of your shortcomings and the shameful things you have done, and I still love you fiercely and relentlessly."

134

What is the appropriate response to this wondrous love? Jesus quoted the Torah's two great commandments: love God with all your heart, soul, mind, and strength, and love your neighbor as you love yourself. Don't miss the fact that you are to "love yourself." Why? Because you were made in God's image and you are loved by God. You have great value in God's eyes.

As my daughters were growing up I felt one of the greatest gifts I could give them was the knowledge that they were dearly loved by their father. My hope was that my love for them would be a reflection of God's love for them. I hoped that if they knew they were loved, they would see their value and worth.

My granddaughter, Stella, knows that she is loved by her grandparents. LaVon and I tell her, and show her, all the time. When she comes to visit, or we go to visit her, the first thing she does is run toward us with her arms up, leaping into our arms. This is, I believe, what God hopes we experience in his love—that we are loved, leading us to reciprocate his love, but also, filled with love, know we have the capacity to love others. As the writer of 1 John 4:11-12 put it: "Beloved, since God loved us so much, we also ought to love one another. No one has ever seen God; if we love one another, God lives in us, and his love is perfected in us" (NRSV).

A Purpose-full Life

When we consider the implications of John 3:16, we find that this verse also offers the answer to the question, "Does my life have purpose?" It affirms that our purpose is both to accept that we are loved and to love God and others. Some people spend an inordinate amount of time trying to figure out the will of God for their lives, as if God had scripted our entire lives in advance. I don't believe God works that way. I believe God created us to

135

make choices and that, while God may know what choices we will make, God takes joy in our making these choices. God's will is less about what school we go to, who we marry, and which career path we take (though each of these decisions may have a path that more closely aligns with God's will), and instead focuses on how we love God and others. If God is love, then we were meant to be, express, and give love, too.

How does that purpose play out in our daily lives? I think we are asked—applying a lesson we learned from the Buddha— to pay attention each day. We are asked to ask ourselves: Who needs love right now? Who needs me to show compassion and mercy? And then, in response, we seek to bless and care for our fellow human beings who need our care.

As one small but concrete example of love in action, every year our church organizes a Super Bowl food drive. Some people get involved by donating sacks of groceries. Some write checks so we can go out and buy entire carts of groceries. Some participate by delivering the groceries to families in the Kansas City area who couldn't afford groceries that month. These are all acts of love. They are all ways to help fulfill our life's purpose.

We hold a blood drive three times a year at the church. Our members see this as a small, concrete expression of what love looks like. It involves taking forty-five minutes away from work and giving a pint of blood for someone whose name you don't even know but who needs what you've offered.

I teach our congregation members to wake up each morning praying, "Lord, use me on your mission today. May my life be lived in response to your love, and as a reflection of your love for others." Expressing this kind of love is meant to be the rhythm of our lives. It gives our lives purpose and meaning. It is who God made us to be.

The Bad News: We Are Perishing

The next phrase of John 3:16 also contains important news for humankind, but it's not so pleasant. It tells us that there is something wrong. Jesus came so that "whosoever believeth in him should not perish, but have everlasting life." Apart from him we will perish. There is more here than meets the eye.

Christians often read this to mean that the human race is destined to perish in hell following our deaths, but Jesus came to provide a way out of hell and to eternal life. The text can mean this. But it's helpful to know that the Greek word for perish is *apollumi*, which is the verb often translated in the Bible as "to destroy." The word can mean a hell after death, but may also mean the kind of destruction humans unleash upon the world and one another in this life.

Both readings of *apollumi* point to the truth that there is something wrong with us. This is the bad news of John 3:16 to which God, out of his love for the world, has responded by giving his "only begotten Son." We must recognize this bad news before we can appreciate the good news.

This thing that is wrong with us that results in destruction or perishing, not only at death but here and now, the Bible calls sin. *Sin* is a word that sounds outdated and preachy, but in the Greek New Testament, as we've learned earlier in this book, it is a really meaningful word. The Greek word is *hamartia*, which means to miss the mark. It is, as you may know, an archery term that describes the shooting of an arrow that misses the target. It was a great metaphor for describing the human condition. We all miss the mark. This further implies that there is a mark or target we should be striving for. As we've seen in several chapters, the Christian mark or ideal is to love God with all that we are, and to love our neighbor as we love ourselves. But we don't

137

always do this. There is something in us that leads us to miss the mark.

This is one of the most incontrovertible assertions of the Christian faith in my opinion. Do you always do the most loving thing for others, or are you ever selfish, or unkind, or even cruel? Do all of your actions reflect your love for God, or do you sometimes do things you know would displease God? The Apostle Paul described the situation by noting, "The desire to do good is inside of me, but I can't do it. I don't do the good that I want to do, but I do the evil that I don't want to do" (Romans 7:18b-19).

It is this missing of the mark that leads to much of the suffering in the world around us. The Seven Deadly Sins, enumerated in some form as early as the fourth century, point to the cardinal sins out of which all others flow. Consider the suffering that results from these sins, listed in order from the least to the most destructive: lust, gluttony, greed, sloth (or indifference), wrath, envy, and the sin the church considered the most deadly, pride. Every war that's ever been fought was motivated by some combination of these. Injustice, abuse, violence, cruelty, genocide, and inhumanity are all rooted in one or more of these.

As a pastor I've listened to many who have confessed to me the sins that they have committed, or shared with me the sins that were committed against them. It is easy to see in the lives of individuals I have known the destruction or perishing that happens as a result of sin this side of death. It's also easy to see when we look at the world around us—thousands of children who die each day without enough food or access to clean drinking water, the oppression, the refugees, the war-torn countries, the dictatorships, and so much more.

Jesus came to save us not only from perishing after death, but to save us from destroying ourselves, others, and the world here and now. In John's Gospel the term "eternal life," or "everlasting life," does not simply refer to heaven or what happens to us when we die. For John, eternal life begins now. It is a quality of life that starts the moment we put our trust in Jesus, yield our lives to him, and seek to follow him.

Lest you doubt that, imagine what our world would be like if every human being loved God and loved one another with the kind of love Jesus offers us. The world would not be perishing or being destroyed. There would be no war, no poverty, no abuse, no violence, no crime, no infidelity, no starvation, no addiction, no loneliness, no feelings of hopelessness. The world would be paradise. God so loved the world that he sent his only begotten Son so that whosoever believeth in him should not perish. He doesn't want us to be destroyed or to destroy. He wants us to find life, and to give life.

We All Know That We Are Broken

Each of the world's great religions recognizes this state of the human condition. In one way or another, they see that we are broken.

Hinduism and Buddhism speak of the law of *karma*, and recognize that human beings have a tendency to produce bad karma by doing what is wrong. These Eastern religions resolve the problem by positing that we are reincarnated again and again, hundreds or perhaps thousands of times, suffering along the way, until, little by little, we relinquish our clinging, we stop inflicting suffering on others, we produce good *karma*, until we finally gain sufficient insight or enlightenment to let go, at which time we are set free.

In Judaism, it is the Law of Moses, as interpreted in the Talmud, that is meant to place humanity on the right track so that we hit the mark. Christians affirm many of those laws, starting with the Ten Commandments and what Jesus identified as the greatest commandments: to love God and to love our neighbor. But the early Christians, who all were Jews, found that, while the Law could point us to the right path, it seemed powerless to help us walk in it. In fact, at times the law actually produces the opposite response: it makes us want to do the very thing it forbids.

Years ago I visited the Hermitage Museum in St. Petersburg, Russia. In one hallway of the museum there was a sculpture by Michelangelo. Amazingly, there were no ropes around it; you could walk right up to it. As I drew closer I saw a sign that said, in multiple languages, "Do not touch." Here's the thing: I had given no thought to touching the statue until I read the sign. It simply had not occurred to me. But the moment I read the prohibition against touching the sculpture, that was all I could think about. I had to suppress the desire to touch it, fearing that I would end up in a Russian jail!

Islam calls its followers to love, and lays out a bit simpler path with five pillars for salvation: submit to God, pray five times a day, give 2.5 percent of your wealth to the poor, fast during daylight hours during the month of Ramadan, and visit Mecca on a pilgrimage at least once in your life. As I noted in the chapter on Islam, thinking about the Five Pillars made me a more devoted Christian, with a greater focus on prayer and Scripture and giving to the poor. But despite doing these things, I'll still wrestle with sin, regularly missing the mark as many Muslims themselves report in describing their own struggles with temptation.

From a Christian perspective, the problem with all of these paths outlined by the different faiths is that they rely on our own feeble attempts to save ourselves by our actions. We are broken, and we cannot rescue or deliver ourselves, no matter how hard we try. The answer is not returning for hundreds or thousands of lifetimes so that we can keep trying to improve. And as important and good as the Law of Moses and the Pillars of Muhammad might be, they, too, cannot rescue us from this deeper human problem.

God Wants to Rescue Us and Make Us Holy People

Though we can't save ourselves, says Christianity, God can save us, and wishes to do so. Why? Because God is love. God is merciful. God actually loves the world. God came in Jesus to show us who he is and what he is like, to help us see his will for our lives, and to show us the mercy he offers us. It's as if God says, "I will forgive you, I will heal you, I will change you from the inside out, I will save you." All that we have to do is accept God's gift of grace and forgiveness; and as we do, we yield our lives to him, inviting God's Spirit to work within us to transform us. All of this is a part of what John means when he writes, "that whosoever believeth in him…" This believing is not merely a mental assent to a set of doctrinal truths. It is trusting in Christ, inviting him to save us, yielding our lives to him as we seek to follow him.

Jesus' life, death, and resurrection are God's answer to our sin, our brokenness, our perishing, our destruction. In Christ we see that God's love for us is so powerful and so steadfast that human brokenness cannot break it. As Christ hangs on the cross, we see the depth of human sin and the magnitude of God's grace. The theologian Paul Tillich once wrote, "Forgiveness is God's answer to the questions implied in our existence." The cross is the answer to the question, "Can I be forgiven?" We hear the answer in Jesus' prayer as he hangs, dying, on the cross: "Father, forgive them, for they know not what they do." The old hymn was right to ask, "What wondrous love is this?"

141

Listen to how Paul expresses this amazing act of redemptive, self-sacrificing love in Ephesians 2:8-10: "You are saved by God's grace because of your faith. This salvation is God's gift. It's not something you possessed. It's not something you did that you can be proud of. Instead, we are God's accomplishment, created in Christ Jesus to do good things. God planned for these good things to be the way that we live our lives."

In Paul's Greek, the word we translate as "accomplishment" is *poiema*, which sounds like the English word for which it is a root: *poem*. We are God's poetry, God's work of art. We were created in Christ Jesus to reflect God's love. God planned for love to be the way we live our lives. As we trust in this love, God's Spirit works in us. And as we seek to follow Christ, we find his love saves us. Our hearts and lives begin to be shaped by love. We come to love God, to love our neighbor, to love even our enemy. We come to love one another as he loved us. We abide in his love. His love abides in our hearts.

When that happens, God sanctifies us—not over the course of thousands of lifetimes but in this one. To sanctify means to *make holy*; he gives us the capacity to walk in the right path, to hit the mark, to live as God intended, and to heal the world.

But What About Heaven?

As noted above, in John's Gospel, everlasting or eternal life is not something we finally attain when we die. We start experiencing eternal life here and now. We experience a bit of heaven on earth. As we live the gospel, we begin to bring heaven here to earth, not only for ourselves but for those around us. But this life certainly extends beyond our death.

The New Testament does not tell us much about what heaven is like. We have images of pearly gates and streets paved with gold, but those are merely meant to suggest that heaven is more beautiful than the most beautiful scenes first-century Christians could imagine.

We can say with confidence that if God is love, and we were made to love, and we are perfected in love through God's grace, then heaven is a place where love is always practiced. It is a place where there is always enough love for everyone, where love is a spring that never runs dry. Heaven is a place where there is no more cruelty, no more hate, no more jealousy or selfishness, no more violence, no more of the pain that comes from feeling unloved. If people don't want to love and experience love always and forever, they can choose to go somewhere besides heaven. Christians call the destination where love for God and others is not practiced, hell. But hell is a choice we make, not one that God wills. God, the Scriptures teach, wants all to be saved from suffering, sorrow, and pain in this life and the next.

Heaven on Earth

We can experience a taste of heaven here and now as we trust in Christ, accepting his love, walking with him and seeking to love God and neighbor. As we do this, we taste a bit of heaven here on earth.

Before his death Jesus said, "I am the resurrection and the life. Whoever believes in me will live, even though they die." He said, "I go to prepare a place for you," and he also said, "I will return and take you to be with me so that where I am you will be too," and "My Father's House has room to spare." I love this picture of heaven!

But it was in his actual resurrection from the dead that these words took on a more profound meaning. In Jesus' suffering and death it seemed that evil, sin, and death had the final word. But that all changed when that first Easter morning the women found his tomb empty, and Jesus appeared in their midst. As

Frederick Buechner once said, Jesus' resurrection made clear that "the worst thing is never the last thing." Hate and violence, evil and suffering—even death—will not have the final word in God's world. No, love has the final word.

The resurrection of Christ answers our last existential question: is there any reason to hope? For Christians, in the light of Easter, there is *always* reason to hope.

That hope is the essence of the Christian gospel. I value Hinduism's emphasis on the transcendent glory of God. I value Buddhism's emphasis on letting go of clinging and on paying attention. I deeply value Judaism's emphasis on doing justice and seeking to be obedient to God. And I find Islam's emphasis on submitting to God of great significance in my own spiritual life. Valuing our common ground allows me to better love my neighbors of other faiths.

Yet as a Christian I believe it is in the life, death, and resurrection of Jesus that God has definitively spoken and offered us a grace, mercy, and love that has the power to save us from our brokenness and to give us life.

Learning from Love

Though I have two degrees in theology, I've often said that I learned more about God by being a father than I learned in college and seminary. Being a parent teaches you something about a kind of love that I couldn't have imagined before my daughters were born.

More recently, I have been learning about God by being a grandfather. One Friday night, we took our granddaughter, Stella, along with her parents on a date to see the film "Peter Rabbit," a contemporary theatrical remake of Beatrix Potter's much loved story. Even though Stella had her own seat, the adults vied for whose lap she would sit on. Eventually, my turn came, and I held Stella tight.

When the movie was over and the credits began to roll, there was music, and that was Stella's cue to say, "C'mon, Papa, let's dance!" Whenever I take Stella to the movies, we have a tradition of dancing to the music at the credits. Usually, we find some quiet place in the back of the theater, or off to the side, where I can twirl Stella around. But on this night, she took my hand and said, "This way, Papa!" as she led me to the front of the theater. So while the theater was emptying, we made our way forward, and we danced in the space between the front row of seats and the screen.

We danced through the first song, and I thought we were done, but the credits continued to roll, as did another song and Stella said, "Papa, let's dance some more!" And so we continued to dance. At the end of that song the lights began to come up, but the credits weren't finished, nor was the music. By this time, the theater was empty except for our family. I said, "Stella, we have to go now. Mimi and Mommy and Daddy want to go home." To which she replied, "Oh, Papa, please! Let's dance for one more song!" and so we did, as the final credits finished rolling. Though she didn't notice, tears streamed down my face as I danced with her. I thought, "I love her so much. I simply couldn't love her more. I'd dance with her forever."

And then it struck me: This love I have for Stella—a willingness to do anything for this child, even lay down my life if I had to— is the kind of love God has for us, the kind of love the Christian gospel was intended to convey. Yes, "God so loves the world that he gave his only begotten son that whosoever believes in him should not perish, but have everlasting life." He loves us relentlessly, fiercely, and he wants us to feel the unbridled joy of a little child, dancing in his arms forever.

An Invitation

My hope is that this book has piqued your interest in learning more about what your neighbors of other faiths believe and why. I hope it has given you tools to start the conversation and to be able to look for and share some of the common ground we have with others. I wrote with the desire that you might be encouraged to reach out and demonstrate love for your neighbors of other faiths. And I hope that by studying other faiths, you might grow deeper in your own faith.

If you are a Christian, I want to encourage you to allow others to see the good news of Jesus Christ lived in tangible ways through you. And, if you are not a Christian and you are interested in knowing more, I'd like to encourage you to visit a church in your community. I happen to be a United Methodist pastor, and there are United Methodist churches in nearly every community in the United States. There are also many other terrific churches in other denominations, as well as non-denominational churches in the US who would welcome you.

Finally, if you've enjoyed this study of other world religions, you might also enjoy my book *Creed*, which was written to explore in depth what Christians believe, why they believe it, and why it matters.

Key Dates Referenced in This Book

Dates	Hinduism	Buddhism
2000 BC	Migration to the Indus River Valley (3000-2000 BC)	
1500 BC		
1400 BC		
1300 BC		
1200 BC		
1100 BC	Vedas composed and passed down orally (2000-1000 BC)	
1000 BC	Vedas committed to writing (1000 BC)	
900 BC		
800 BC		
700 BC		
600 BC		
	Earliest Upanishads composed (600 BC)	Siddhartha Gautama is born (563 BC)
		Siddhartha leaves home to become a monk at age 29 (534 BC)
	Bhagavad Gita written (550-500 BC)	Siddhartha attains enlightenment and becomes the Buddha (528 BC)
500 BC		

Islam	Judaism	Christianity
	Abraham and Sarah (ca. 2000 BC)	Abraham and Sarah (ca. 2000 BC)
	Moses leads the Israelites out of slavery in Egypt (+/- 1300 BC)	Moses leads the Israelites out of slavery in Egypt (+/- 1300 BC)
	King David (ca. 1000 BC)	King David (ca. 1000 BC)
	Hebrew prophets (850-450 BC)	Hebrew prophets (850-450 BC)
	Jerusalem and the Temple destroyed (587 BC)	Jerusalem and the Temple destroyed (587 BC)
	Babylonian Exile (586-539 BC)	Babylonian Exile (586-539 BC)
	Second Temple is built (520-515 BC)	Second Temple is built (520-515 BC)

Key Dates Referenced in This Book

Dates	Hinduism	Buddhism
400 BC		Siddhartha Gautama dies (483 BC)
100 BC		Pali Canon committed to writing (1st century BC)
0		
AD 100		
AD 200		
AD 300		
AD 400		

Islam	Judaism	Christianity
	Ezra and Nehemiah (ca. 450-400 BC)	Ezra and Nehemiah (ca. 450-400 BC)
		Life of Jesus (4 BC-AD 29)
		Jesus is crucified (AD 29/30)
	Destruction of the Temple (AD 70)	Paul's missionary journeys and letters (AD 45-65)
	Development of oral law (pre-539 BC-AD 200)	Gospels committed to writing (AD 70-100)
	Mishnah is written and codified (ca. AD 70-200)	
		Council of Nicea (AD 325)
		General Agreement on NT canon (ca. AD 350-382)
	Jerusalem Talmud (ca. AD 350-400)	St. Jerome (AD 347-420)
		Vulgate completed (ca. AD 400)
		St. Augustine (AD 354-430)
		Council of Chalcedon (AD 451)

Key Dates Referenced in This Book

Dates	Hinduism	Buddhism
AD 500		
AD 600		
AD 700		

Islam	Judaism	Christianity
	Babylonian Talmud (ca. AD 500)	Council of Chalcedon (AD 451)
		Second Council of Constantinople (AD 553)
uhammad is born D 570)		Pope Gregory the Great (AD 590-604)
uhammad marries at e 25 (AD 595)		
uhammad visited by abriel and begins recit- g the Quran (AD 610)		
uhammad teaches the essages he receives D 610-632)		
uhammad moves to edina (ca. AD 622)		
uhammad captures ecca (AD 629)		
uhammad dies D 632)		Third Council of Constantinople (AD 680-681)
lam spreads rapidly D 632-750)		
		Crusades (AD 1095-1291)

NOTES

Chapter 1

1. "The Changing Global Religious Landscape," Pew Research Center, April 5, 2017, http://www.pewforum.org/2017/04/05/the-changing-global-religious-landscape/, accessed June 25, 2018.

2. Walter Chalmers Smith, "Immortal, Invisible, God Only Wise," in *The United Methodist Hymnal* (Nashville: The United Methodist Publishing House, 1989), 103.

3. C. S. Lewis, *The Last Battle* (New York: HarperCollins, 1994), 205–206.

Chapter 2

1. Carol Kuruvilla, "Widow of Kansas Hate Crime Victim Makes Touching Plea for the New Year," Huffington Post, January 2, 2018, https://www.huffingtonpost.com/entry/sunayana-dumala-embrace-diversity-new-year_us_5a4b9c5ee4b025f99e1db870, accessed June 26, 2018.

Chapter 4

1. Judy L. Thomas, "'Curse of covenant' persists—restrictive rules, while unenforceable, have lingering legacy," *The Kansas City Star*, July 27, 2016, http://www.kansascity.com/news/local/article92156112.html#storylink=cpy, accessed June 27, 2018.

2. Michael Kunzelman, "Report: Anti-Semitic Incidents Soar by 57 Percent in 2017," Associated Press, February 27, 2018, https://apnews.com/caf56960410f4422a8db19cb996365e9, accessed June 27, 2018.

3. Robert Robinson, "Come, Thou Fount of Every Blessing," in *The United Methodist Hymnal* (Nashville: The United Methodist Publishing House, 1989), 400.

Chapter 5

1. "U.S. Anti-Muslim Hate Crimes Rose 15 Percent in 2017: Advocacy Group," Reuters, April 23, 2018, https://www.reuters.com/article/us-usa-islam-hatecrime/u-s-anti-muslim-hate-crimes-rose-15-percent-in-2017-advocacy-group-idUSKBN1HU240, accessed June 28, 2018.

2. "A Covenant Prayer in the Wesleyan Tradition," *The United Methodist Hymnal*, 607.

3. AJ Willingham, Paul Martucci and Natalie Leung, "The chances of a refugee killing you - and other surprising immigration stats," CNN, March 6, 2017, https://www.cnn.com/2017/01/30/politics/immigration-stats-by-the-numbers-trnd/index.html, accessed June 28, 2018.

4. Emmanuelle Saliba, "You're More Likely to Die Choking Than Be Killed by Foreign Terrorists, Data Show," NBC News, February 1, 2017, https://www.nbcnews.com/news/us-news/you-re-more-likely-die-choking-be-killed-foreign-terrorists-n715141, accessed June 28, 2018.

5. David Neiwert, Darren Ankrom, Esther Kaplan and Scott Pham, "Homegrown Terror: Explore 9 years of domestic terrorism plots and attacks," *Reveal* (from The Center for Investigative Reporting), June 22, 2017, https://apps.revealnews.org/homegrown-terror/, accessed June 28, 2018.

FOR FURTHER STUDY

E. Stanley Jones. *The Christ of the Indian Road*. Nashville: Abingdon Press, 1925.

Paul F. Knitter. *Introducing Theologies of Religions*. Maryknoll, NY: Orbis, 2002.

Marion H. Larsen and Sara L. H. Shady. *From Bubble to Bridge: Educating Christians for a Multifaith World*. Downers Grove, IL: IVP Academic, 2017.

Eboo Patel. *InterFaith Leadership: A Primer*. Boston: Beacon Press, 2016.

Jennifer Howe Peace, Or N. Rose, and Greg Mobley, eds. *My Neighbor's Faith: Stories of Interreligious Encounter, Growth, and Transformation*. Maryknoll, NY: Orbis, 2012.

Stephen Prothero. *God Is Not One: The Eight Rival Religions That Run the World*. New York: HarperOne, 2010.

Huston Smith. *The World's Religions: Our Great Wisdom Traditions*. New York: HarperOne, 1991.

Krista Tippett. *Speaking of Faith: Why Religion Matters—and How to Talk About It*. New York: Penguin, 2008.

ACKNOWLEDGMENTS

There are so many people who played a part in creating this new revised edition of *Christianity and World Religions*, and I want to acknowledge them here. While this is a new edition of my 2005 book by the same name, in many ways we started from scratch in creating this book. As with many of my books, this one began as a sermon series. In that series, I sought to teach the people of The United Methodist Church of the Resurrection how to have meaningful conversations with people of other faiths and to help them understand what others believe, why they believe it, where we find common ground, and where we will simply always disagree. Special thanks to the people of Resurrection for being the kind of congregation that makes it possible for me to preach sermons like this and to prepare books and resources like the one you are holding.

I'd like to thank my assistant, Sue Thompson, for helping me keep the plates spinning in my chaotic life. Cathy Bien, our director of communications, helped line up interviews with leaders of other faiths in Kansas City. Sandy Thailing, Lee Rudeen, Greg Hoeven, and Kersee Meyer filmed interviews with these faith leaders for use in the sermons. Some of these clips also appear in the small group videos that are available for this book.

Special thanks to Matt and Sangeeta Kleinman, Dr. Debabrata Bhaduri, Venerable Urgyen Pete Machik Potts, Rabbi Art Nemitoff, and Sheikh Dahee Saeed, who each graciously allowed me to interview them for this book. I am grateful for their time, their hospitality, and their kindness as I interviewed them for this project.

I'm grateful for the team at Abingdon who wished to release a new edition of this book and their work on preparing the initial draft based upon my sermons. Susan Salley heads the team and is a tremendous gift to me. Ron Kidd, who recently retired from Abingdon, has been my editor for fourteen years. He has been an important partner in most of the books I've written over the last fourteen years and in the editing of the small group videos. I'm grateful to have Brian Sigmon stepping into Ron's role. Ron worked on the first draft of this manuscript, and Brian took over in editing my second draft and the videos. Also on the Abingdon team, I want to acknowledge Tim Cobb, Marcia Myatt, Alan Vermilye, Laura Lockhart, Tracey Craddock, Trey Ward, and the many others who helped produce this book.

Finally, I want to thank LaVon Bandy Hamilton, my wife of 36 years, who has been my muse, my best friend, and my conversation partner on every book I've written including this one.

Adam Hamilton
July 2018